**Longman Handbooks for Language Teachers**

D0781241

# Process Writing

Ron White
Valerie Arndt

**Longman**
**London and New York**

# Acknowledgements

Many of the sources of inspiration for this book will be obvious from the Bibliography. Less obvious, but of equal importance, are the colleagues and students who have provided texts and ideas. Among the teachers who have contributed are Maggie Charles, Norman Coe, Rosemary Dorie, Elizabeth Goletti, Michele Guerrini, Charles Hadfield, Stephen Keeler, Maria Auxiliardora Keller, Jonathan Marks, Sue Robson, Tony Shannon-Little and Alan Tonkyn. To them, to our students and to others unnamed, we express our gratitude.

Ron White
Valerie Arndt

We are grateful to the following for permission to reproduce copyright material:
Action Publications for an extract from the article 'Marriage Lines' from *Sunjet*, Cyprus Airways in-flight magazine, Vol 5, No 7, Summer 1988; EFL Gazette for the article 'Obituary for Raymond Tongue' from *EFL Gazette*; the author, Timothy J Greenwood, for an adapted extract from his article 'Artist among the gorillas' from *Country Life* 26.5.88; the author, Peter Guttridge, for his article 'Abbey Rebels Aim For Seats On Board' from *The Independent Magazine* 1.4.89; The Hunger Project for an extract from the report *World Development Forum*; Ewan MacNaughton Associates for extracts from the articles 'My Country Right or Wrong?' from *Telegraph Sunday Magazine* 20.12.87 & 'My Country Right or Wrong?' from *Telegraph Sunday Magazine* 11.1.87, (c) Telegraph Sunday Magazine & the extract 'The Postcard' from *The First Book of Mini-Sagas* by G Carter (pub Alan Sutton Publishing Ltd, 1985), (c) The Daily Telegraph plc & Alan Sutton Publishing Ltd; New Internationalist Publications Ltd for the letter 'Cow Freaks' by J Nebel from *New Internationalist* 183, May 1988 & the article 'The loss of Lardie Moonlight' from *New Internationalist* 191, January 1989; Newspaper Publishing plc for extracts from the article 'Camera Woman' by Bruce Bernard from *The Independent Magazine* 18.3.89, an adapted extract from the article 'Turning the Alps into a rocky desert' by Patricia Clough from *The Independent* 16.1.88, the article 'Still lives of Liscannor' by Peter Dunn from *The Independent Magazine* 25.2.89, the article 'British haven for people of Hong Kong ruled out' by Colin Hughes from *The Independent* 7.6.89 & an extract from the article 'Language of lawyers explained' by Miles Kington from *The Independent* June 1989; Newspaper Publishing plc on behalf of the authors for letters by Anderson & T Brown from *The Independent* 10.3.89, a letter by The Rev R H Darroch from *The Independent* 15.3.89, a letter by A Elletson from *The Independent* 14.3.89, a letter by T Godfrey from *The Independent* 10.3.89, a letter by A Hiscox from *The Independent* 22.3.89, a letter by L & G Jukes from *The Independent* 15.3.89, a letter by C Mainstone from *The Independent* 8.3.89, a letter by J Plumptre from *The Independent* 13.3.89; the author, Kenneth Quicke (Ken Pursey) for his letter from *Country Life* 20.10.88; Today newspaper for the article 'Maggie lets in the rich' from *Today* 7.6.89.

We have been unable to trace the copyright holder in the following & would appreciate any information that would enable us to do so:
the article 'Ghost Story' by Jane Dent; the article 'My Country Right or Wrong?' from *Telegraph Sunday Magazine* 13.12.87.

We are grateful to the following for their permission to reproduce photographs and other copyright material:

Colorific / Alfred Eisenstaedt / Life Magazine © Time Warner Inc, for page 98. Greg Evans Photo Library for page 65 (bottom right). Fabian Carlsson Gallery / Andy Goldsworthy for page 65 (bottom left). Bruce Gilbreth Architects Limited for page 65 (top). Greenpeace UK for page 71 (bottom). Impact Photos / Penny Tweedie for page 146. The Independent for page 90 (middle). George Kavanagh for page 153. Magdalene College for page 62. Magnum Photos, Inc / © Elliot Erwitt for page 36 (bottom). New Internationalist for pages 51 and 60 / Steve Weston for page 61. Ocean Images, Inc / Al Giddings for page 71 (top right). Pirelli UK PLC for page 68. Popperfoto for pages 36 (top) and 37. Today / News UK Limited for page 90 (top).

We are unable to trace the copyright holder of the photograph on page 71 (top left), and would be grateful for any information which would enable us to do so.

# Contents

(▶ and ○: see Introduction p. 9)

# Introduction

**Our aims in writing this book**

Almost two thousand years ago, the great Chinese writer, Lu Chi, reflecting in his essay *Wen Fu* (The Art of Letters)* upon the process of writing and being a writer, acknowledged the power of the written word:

> '*Behold now the utility of letters . . .*
> *It extends over a thousand miles and nothing can stop its course;*
> *It penetrates a million years, the ferry from one to the other . . .*'

It is precisely this capacity of written language to transcend time and space that makes the teaching and learning of writing such an important experience. Through writing we are able to share ideas, arouse feelings, persuade and convince other people. We are able to discover and articulate ideas in ways that only writing makes possible.

Yet despite the power of writing – as a permanent record, as a form of expression and as a means of communication – it has tended to be a much neglected part of the language programme, both in first and foreign or second language teaching. This book is an attempt to redress that imbalance, and to provide a stimulus to teachers and students for collaborating on a series of valuable educational experiences.

Our intention has been to provide a resource book comprising a collection of procedures and lesson formats – or 'templates' – and, although much exemplification is provided, you will find that this book does not contain a large quantity of textual material because it is primarily about writing activities. Priority is given to the students creating their own texts, rather than having them analyse finished products of other writers. This does not mean that we ignore the importance of reading for writing development, or of becoming familiar with the conventions of text-types. Rather, we try to put such things in perspective as only some among many ways of developing writing proficiency.

To give tangible form to the activities we have included two types of exemplification. One type is authentic student writing, illustrating what might be anticipated as output from the activity concerned. These examples are presented 'warts and all', without corrections to language or spelling. The second type consists of input texts which could be used as they are, as stimulus material for a lesson or series of lessons, though they are primarily intended as a guide to the kind of material which could be exploited. The rationale for this

---

* Lu Chi's essay also provides the superscriptions for each section of our book.

1

is that we feel it wrong for us to dictate to your students what they should write about. We want you to choose from and adapt the procedures we have outlined in ways which match your students' needs and interests. Moreover, the process of composing is highly individualistic, and writers need to draw upon a variety of techniques which they find useful for themselves.

Think of this book, if you like, as a collection of 'recipes'. As in a recipe book, ingredients and procedures are indicated, but the user has to provide, combine and prepare the actual materials. And, as in cooking, where individual cooks produce their own variations on a given recipe, so too in this book we want to encourage you and your students to work out your own methods of exploiting the formats we have offered. Thus, the way in which procedures are used will vary from class to class according to the different ingredients and methods you choose. Indeed, we believe it to be essential that teachers adapt – or 're-invent' – any teaching procedure in ways which are appropriate for them and their students. One cannot, as a teacher, be said to 'own' any teaching procedure until it has been adapted to one's own style and circumstance, just as any cook adapts a recipe to the conditions under which a dish is to be prepared.

Clearly, it would be difficult and possibly counterproductive to cover all the activities outlined here during a typical school writing programme, with its constraints of time and syllabus. Some activities will prove more useful, appealing or productive than others. What we hope is that, through experimentation, teachers and students will be able to develop a broad repertoire of activities based on the outlines and examples given in this book.

## Our assumptions about teaching writing

The proposals we make in this book are based on the assumption that teaching and learning are joint enterprises involving both teacher and students in a partnership where the participants have complementary roles and similar status. This calls for a change in role relationship between teacher and taught, and has considerable consequences. It means, for one thing, that there are greater risks on both sides. The teacher, instead of being cast merely in the role of linguistic judge, now becomes a reader, responding to what the students have written; the students, rather than merely providing evidence of mastery of linguistic forms, proffer experiences, ideas, attitudes and feelings to be shared with a reader. This will, inevitably, involve some degree of self-disclosure in which teachers and students move beyond a conventional, relatively impersonal teacher-student relationship into territory where different rules apply. This is clearly the case in responding to the writer of *My most unforgettable character*, given as an example of student writing in 6.2 *Responding* (p. 124). Here there is a degree of self-disclosure which the teacher-reader can hardly ignore, and simply to treat such a piece of writing as a display of language proficiency would not only constitute a denial of the trust which the writer had placed in the teacher-reader, but would also be against the philosophy which lies behind the approach we advocate.

Indeed, treating any piece of writing primarily as a source of language errors misses the point of our approach. Grammar is important – but as a tool, a means, and not as an end in itself. Such research evidence as we have suggests that focusing on language errors in writing improves neither grammatical accuracy nor writing fluency. So, the activities in this book are based on the assumption that it is through attention to meaning, and not just form, that language – and writing – improve.

Moving into such uncharted territory can, we realise from our own teaching experience, be threatening. But we are also convinced that there is much to be gained from it. If, as in 2.1.1 *Brainstorming by the teacher*, 3.1.2 *Loopwriting by the teacher*, and 5.1 *Drafting by the teacher* (pp. 19, 47, 100), a collaborative, workshop atmosphere between teacher and students is developed, such threat is soon forgotten in the process of joint composing and responding.

Finally, we believe that writing takes time. In particular, time is needed to incubate, sift and shape ideas. We also know that time is one of the most precious resources of both teachers and students and that when, as is often the case, time is at a premium, writing is one of the first things to be cut back or relegated to homework. Yet, of all the skills, writing is the one which most needs and benefits from time. So, we advocate devoting classroom time to writing. As it happens, many of the activities we have suggested in this book involve pair and group work, not to mention discussion and collaboration, so that the writing class becomes, in a very genuine sense, a communicative experience in which much more than skill in writing is practised and developed.

**Our assumptions about writing**

Writing is far from being a simple matter of transcribing language into written symbols: it is a thinking process in its own right. It demands conscious intellectual effort, which usually has to be sustained over a considerable period of time. Furthermore, precisely because cognitive skills are involved, proficiency in language does not, of itself, make writing easier. People writing in their native language, though they may have a more extensive stock of language resources to call upon, frequently confront exactly the same kinds of writing problems as people writing in a foreign or second language.

In order to think of effective ways of coming to grips with these problems, we have to find out what actually goes on when people write. And this is notoriously difficult. Much of the evidence that we do have has been obtained from various kinds of observations of writers at work, and introspections of writers themselves, as in the 'compose aloud' activities described in 1 *Glimpsing the process* (pp. 11–16). What the transcripts from such activities help reveal is that there is much more to writing than a mere learning and applying of linguistic or rhetorical rules. Rather, writing is a form of problem-solving which involves such processes as generating ideas, discovering a 'voice' with which to write, planning, goal-setting, monitoring and evaluating what is going to be written as well as what has been written, and searching for language with which to express exact meanings. Moreover, writers rarely know at the outset exactly what it is they are going to write because many ideas are only revealed during the act of writing itself.

We have attempted to visualise our perception of writing processes, as derived from such research, in *Figure 1* on the next page. Here the complex and recursive nature of writing is displayed. Obviously, this model is a gross simplification of the highly intricate, dynamic and constantly fluctuating interplay of activities involved in writing, but it may serve as a framework into which individual facets of the overall process can be fitted, while also acting as a guide to the organisation of this book. This model has been amended from

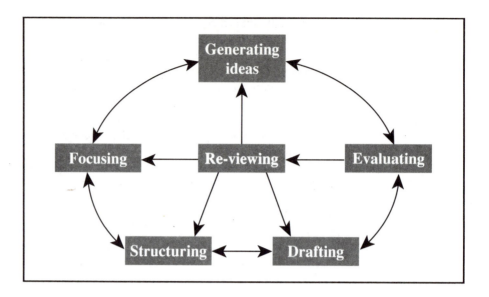

*Figure 1: A model of writing*

the first printing as a result of constructive comments from our readers.

As will be obvious from this model, writers are faced with a very complex management problem because they are darting back and forth from one process to another in real time, and at each point they have to make decisions at all levels, whether at the level of ideas, of planning, of organising or of expression. Furthermore, there is interaction among the different processes such that some processes occur simultaneously, with one influencing another.

A second challenging task which writers face is that they have to organise an amorphous mass of ideas, information and associations into coherent, linear text. Moreover, they can neither speak to nor see the person or persons they are addressing. All they have to convey their message is the abstract symbol system of written language. With this, they must make explicit every aspect of their meaning; their text must create its own context.

At the same time, writers have to consider what we might call the 'laws of communication'. Whenever we engage in any kind of communication which requires language, we operate within a framework of unspoken rules or conventions. Thus, readers expect that writers will give them neither more nor less information than is needed for the message to be understood. They assume, too, that writers will not give them information which they know to be false, or for which they lack sufficient evidence, or which is irrelevant to their purpose in writing. And finally, readers expect writers to use language which is clear, unambiguous, and appropriate to the context and type of text concerned. If writers deliberately flout these unwritten laws, they do so in order to make some kind of extraordinary impact on their readers. If, however, they simply fail to observe these conventions, they produce writing which is unsatisfactory and ineffective.

It is easy to neglect these 'laws' when we write, for the nature of writing is such that it engrosses us in our own thought processes, and carries us off into a mental world where there is no feedback from a present audience. Thus, as writers, we need to make a constant and conscious effort to imagine our intended readers and anticipate their reactions to the symbols we have put on the page. We have to evaluate, for instance, how much knowledge we share with our readers, and how much is exclusive to us; we must decide how to 'package' our information to achieve our purpose in writing; we have to judge whether the language we have chosen conveys the whole of our meaning; and we need to make sure that readers will be able to follow the train of thought underpinning the whole text.

**Our focus on process writing**

Essentially, we see a process-focused approach to writing as an *enabling* approach. In this, we have been influenced by the work of many other researchers and teachers, amongst them Peter Elbow, Donald Graves, Linda Flower and John Hayes, Vivien Zamel, Ann Raimes, and Carl Bereiter and Marlene Scardamalia, to mention just a few (See Bibliography (pp. 186). As we see it, the goal of this approach is to nurture the skills with which writers *work out their own solutions to the problems they set themselves*, with which they shape their raw material into a coherent message, and with which they work towards an acceptable and appropriate form for expressing it.

Such an approach views all writing – even the most mundane and routine – as creative. The writer, and the writer alone, is responsible for the text which eventually evolves from the raw material, no matter whether that material is generated almost entirely from the writer's imagination (as in, say, writing a short story), or whether, at the other extreme, it is provided almost entirely from external sources (as in, for instance, writing a report).

What is important for us as teachers of writing is to engage our students in that creative process; to excite them about how their texts are coming into being; to give them insights into how they operate as they create their work; to alter their concepts of what writing involves. What we have to get across is the notion that writing is *re*-writing; that *re*-vision – seeing with new eyes – has a central role to play in the act of creating a text, and is not merely a boring error-checking exercise; and above all, that evaluation is not just the province of the teacher alone at the final stage of the process, but that it is equally the concern and responsibility of the writer at *every* stage.

What we most certainly do not mean to imply by advocating such an approach, however, is a repudiation of all interest in the product (i.e. the final draft). On the contrary, the main aim is to arrive at the best product possible. What differentiates a process-focused approach from a product-centred one, though, is that the outcome of writing – that is, the product – is not preconceived. Writing in a process approach is divergent, with as many different outcomes as there are writers. In a typical product-centred approach, on the other hand, writing will converge towards a pre-defined goal, with a model text being presented to form the focus of comprehension and text manipulation activities. What will not be obvious in this latter approach, either from the model text, or from the activities based on it, is *how* the writer actually composed it. By contrast, process-focused lessons may introduce texts written by other people, but only *after* the students have written something of their own, so that the text is now a resource for further ideas rather than a model for mimicry.

It is as well to remember, though, that whatever the enthusiasm and commitment generated by a process approach, neither teachers nor students should expect sudden miracles to occur, such that elementary students suddenly become intermediate level writers as a result of the activities they have engaged in. Indeed, it would be unreasonable to expect such transformations to occur. What process-focused activities will do is help students develop in ways which are appropriate to and fulfilling for their level of language proficiency. More than that cannot be expected.

Disorder, imprecision, recursiveness, complexity, individual variation – this is the very stuff of a process-oriented approach to writing. And the more we find out about what writers actually do when they write, the more comprehensive a specification of writing skills we shall be able to develop, and in turn, a more flexible and adaptable range of teaching techniques. This is especially important in the context of foreign or second language teaching, where writing has often tended to be used as a vehicle for little more than either language-learning reinforcement or for the display of linguistic proficiency. What we, as teachers, should be aiming at is creating an environment in which our students, rather than being intimidated and frustrated by the complexity of writing, are engaged in and enthused by it, and where they feel that credit is given for every aspect of the effort which goes into the writing process. Our goal is to present writing as a stimulating process centred upon, as Lu Chi put it, the 'matching of matter and manner' such that it becomes 'the ferry' between the writer and the reader.

**Notes on using the book**

Our book takes as its organising principle the various processes entailed in the act of writing. This means that each of the six main sections of the book groups together activities centred on one of these processes: *Generating, Focusing, Structuring, Drafting, Evaluating* and *Re-viewing*. Since these operations apply to the creation of any piece of writing, irrespective of text-type or subject matter, the idea is that the procedures suggested can be used with any text which teachers and/or students decide upon, according to the level, interests and requirements of each teaching context. Thus we have suggested neither text-type nor level for any of the units, though clearly some will lend themselves more readily to certain types of writing than others, and some, which require a fairly sophisticated language base to start from – many of the units in 7.4 *Assessing impact* (p. 156), for instance – will obviously be inappropriate for lower level classes. You will also find that with a few exceptions there are no specific indications as to time allowed for each activity. Choice of materials, learner enthusiasm and timetabling constraints must dictate this according to individual circumstances.

The writing process is a recursive one, in which the activities we have had to group and present in some kind of linear order in this book do not occur in any fixed sequence in the act of creating a text – though in most cases there will obviously tend to be more generating and focusing activities at the outset, and more emphasis on evaluating and re-viewing as the drafting progresses. The sequence of activities as presented in the book is not, therefore, necessarily one to be rigidly kept to in the writing programme which you, the individual teacher, will devise.

However, although we have left it up to you to decide how and in which order to use the activities suggested, we do advocate planning a series of lessons around the particular writing assignment you have in mind, which will draw upon a selection of tasks from various sections. Thus your students may end up writing fewer essays per term or course than customary, but these pieces of work will have had the chance of being carefully thought out and worked through. A typical sequence of activities would probably look something like this:

Discussion (class, small group, pair)
   Brainstorming/making notes/asking questions
      Fastwriting/selecting ideas/establishing a viewpoint
         Rough draft
           Preliminary self-evaluation
             Arranging information/structuring the text
           First draft
             Group/peer evaluation and responding
            Conference
           Second draft
             Self-evaluation/editing/proof-reading
           Finished draft
            Final responding to draft

Although, as we have been at pains to point out, dramatic transformations will not necessarily result from persuading students to adopt such a plan of attack upon a piece of writing, you may be surprised at the sorts of improvements which sensitive responding and at least two drafts may lead to. On the next page, for instance, is an essay on the topic *Shopping* produced by Mitsuo Toki, an eighteen-year-old Japanese student, during his first two weeks on a language course in Britain. You will see his first draft, then the teacher's response to it, and finally the finished version (in this case his third draft). It is worth noting, incidentally, that when this essay was marked, credit was given for all three drafts.

**Draft 1**

> Reather and food is very prise down.
> Shop's man is careful.
> Always very prise down.
> I went to shopping for three days;.
> I want to buy sheet.
> If my room is very cold in the morning.
> I don't understand that English shop rest on Sunday.
> Japanese shop don't understand and impossible.
> I bought the bicycle on Saturday.
> It's 120£ and black color.
> It's very nice.
> But I ride its.
> Because it was stolen on Sunday.
> I have to the o'clock.
> Because it was broken.
> Only shopping may not speak English.

**Teacher's response**

Dear Mitsuo,

I am interested to learn that you think leather goods and food are cheap in England. Are they cheaper than in Japan? Can you give examples of the differences in price?

I am not surprised that you found it necessary to buy a *blanket* (not a sheet – sheets are made of cotton and are not warm) because of the cold weather.

You find the shopping hours unusual. For some years, there have been attempts to change the shopping hours. In Scotland, for instance, shops are open on Sundays. And even in England, some shops are open.

What do you mean by: *Japanese shop don't understand and impossible?*

I was very sorry indeed to learn that your new bicycle was stolen. Unfortunately, you have to be very, very careful with bicycles and other things. Did you lock your bicycle? If you don't lock your bicycle with a good chain and lock, it will be stolen, as you have discovered.

Did you ride your bicycle before it was stolen? Did you go anywhere on your bicycle?

What do you mean by: *I have to the o'clock?* And you say: *Because it was broken.* What was broken? Do you mean that your alarm clock was broken?

You also say: *Only shopping may not speak English.*
I am not sure what you mean by this. Can you explain?

Can you rewrite your essay on shopping, answering some of my questions? Also, refer to your *English Grammar in Use*, Unit 61.4, for the correct pattern for the verb *shop*.

Yours,
(the teacher)

**Draft 3**

I like shopping in England. Because leather and food are very inexpensive. But maybe this is only Japanese sense. For instance, for leather jacket of same quality, the Japanese price is about £500, but English price is about 100£. What a difference price it is!

I have been to shopping for three days. I want to buy a bedding because my room is very cold in the morning. Next then I want to buy a new clock because my old clock was broken when my suitcase was dropped by the airline . I bought a bicycle on Sunday. It's 120£ and black colour and very nice but I ride it only one day because it was stolen on Sunday. I don't know why English shops rest on Sunday. Japanese shops don't understand and impossible.

But I like shopping. Shopping is easy because I can use gestures instead at speaking English.

*Figure 2: Mitsuo Toki's 'Shopping' essay*

The sequence of activities suggested on p. 7 will probably – with variations – form the basis of your lesson planning. However, you may also find that your teaching context allows you the opportunity to devote a series of lessons from time to time to a particular aspect of the writing process – *Assessing impact*, perhaps, or *Considering audience*, or *Checking connections*. In this case, you would probably use a series of tasks from these particular units.

Not all units and not all activities are concerned with actual writing tasks. Those which do not come under the 'getting on with the job' label fall into two categories. In the first category (marked ○) are *'sensitising'* tasks, and in the second category (marked ▶) are *'techniques'* for applying the approach we are advocating.

The 'sensitising' units are aimed at increasing students' awareness of what is involved in writing – the importance of taking purpose or audience into account, for instance, or recognising typical features of different kinds of writing. The introductory unit, 1 *Glimpsing the process*, is a sensitising activity of a different kind, suggesting a way of giving students an insight into what they actually do when they write. While this could be useful as an introduction to a writing course with a group of advanced students, it would probably be daunting to lower level groups, and would be more valuable at a later stage, once they had become more confident with the language.

The 'techniques' units address teaching technique rather than give suggestions for student activities; they are concerned with ways of applying the philosophy of the process-focused approach. We believe, for instance, that it is important for teachers to do some writing in the classroom – hence the various 'teacher-fronted' activities such as 2.1.1 *Brainstorming by the teacher*, 3.1.2 *Loopwriting by the teacher* and 5.1 *Drafting by the teacher*. These activities can all be carried out very satisfactorily on the board or OHP. However, if you have access to a video rig and word processor you can make them even more effective. Set up the word processor so that you face the class and can talk to your students as you write, and have the video camera trained over your shoulder onto the computer screen, linked to a large monitor or VDU visible to the class; or, if your computer can be directly linked to the VDU facing the students, you can dispense with the video camera. This technique will enable your students to see exactly what you do as you write, and you can talk your process through with them, explaining the decisions you are making, and asking for suggestions when you get stuck.

Another cornerstone of our philosophy is that it is essential to create time to discuss each student's writing with them in a face-to-face situation, and not merely to provide one-way written feedback in the form of 'marking'. Hence units 6.2 *Responding* and 6.3 *Conferencing*. It is not always easy to find enough time to have individual consultations with every student, but if you make it the norm that a lot of writing is actually done in the writing classroom, not only will you be able to talk to individual students about their writing whilst others are working on other tasks, but you will also be able to monitor work in progress more effectively.

A final point concerns the publishing of students' writing. We believe that writing should be a means of discovering ideas, sharing opinions, presenting information, arousing a response from the reader, and even entertaining. In many of the activities we have outlined, you will find that students exchange, read, respond to and discuss each other's work. In addition to this, though, we would like to suggest that, wherever feasible, the outcomes of a series of lessons centred on the production of a certain text should be 'published' – that is to say, made public. There are many ways of doing this. Make a wall or board display; or collect articles and essays in a class magazine; or create files devoted to different themes or topics. Or, with some administrative flexibility and ingenuity, it is possible to arrange for different classes to swap texts. Each class responds to the other's work as readers, and the exercise becomes a very effective way of finding out if the writers have been successful in conveying their message. All these are means of persuading students that writing, though difficult and demanding, can be exciting, challenging and rewarding.

# 1

# Glimpsing the process

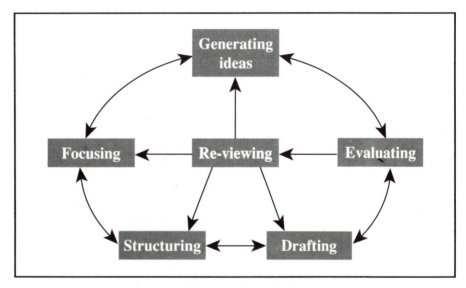

*'He stilled the waters of his mind to stabilise his thinking; he peered into his thoughts and one by one put them into words . . .'*

## Composing aloud ○

For many students, writing is a chore to be got through for a grade, and to many others, not only is it a chore, but a boring one at that. Comments such as the following – all of them from EFL students on writing in English – will be familiar to us:

> 'Oh, I've no ideas . . .'
> 'It is always not enjoyable to get it started . . .'
> 'If there is any satisfaction, it comes only at the end . . .'
> 'I don't think writing is a very satisfactory experience, because it takes a lot of time and also requires a lot of effort . . .'
> 'The trouble is that people usually judge your knowledge by what you can write . . .'

We believe that there is no point in pretending that writing is easy. Indeed, certain cognitive psychologists have described it as the most complex and demanding of all cognitive activities undertaken by human beings, because there are no rules (see Bracewell (1981)). Writers are free agents: they can choose to say what they want, how they want.

However, we also believe that writing can be exciting, precisely because of this freedom, and at the same time immensely satisfying. It is, after all, an act of creation. And because, as one of the students above pointed out, we are often judged by our writing, our responsibility as teachers of writing is to see that our students learn to write as effectively and successfully as possible. Perhaps they may even find it, eventually, a challenging and rewarding experience.

Most people have probably never asked themselves exactly what they do when they write. Nor is it likely they will ever know, because writing is essentially a thinking process, and certain aspects of thought are inaccessible to consciousness. Some surface manifestations of the writing process can be glimpsed, though, and since this book is organised around the various procedures we engage in during the process of writing, we thought it appropriate to start with an activity known as 'composing aloud' which might help students to become aware of what is going on when they write.

Written thought is often meagre in comparison with the wealth of mental effort that went into producing it; and we, as writers, often find it frustrating that the reader fails to understand or follow from the written page the meaning which is so clear to us. Composing aloud is an attempt to recreate the thought processes which underlie a piece of written text. It involves verbalising thought – or thinking aloud – as one writes. Not only can it help to reconstruct the thinking that went into the writing, and thus supply important clues for improving the coherence of the text; it can also give us a fascinating insight into what goes on as we struggle to translate meaning into words.

**Procedure**

1 It is easiest to set this activity up in the language laboratory (although you can do it with tape-recorders, if necessary). You will first need to give your students some idea about what it entails.

**Aims·**
(a) To give an insight into what is involved in the writing process.
(b) To help reconstruct the train of thought which underlies the text they will write.

**How to proceed**:
Tell your students that although it is an unnatural task, they have to try to verbalise as much as possible of what goes on in their mind *as they write*, including seemingly irrelevant things.

**Language**:
They can verbalise their thoughts in whatever language they wish, although they should write in English. The important thing is to keep talking, and the taped 'composing aloud' is for their ears only.

Since this will probably be a novel activity for most students, get them perhaps to do a trial run for ten minutes or so, to get used to the idea. Or, record yourself composing, and play the tape to introduce the activity.

2 Students then do their composing aloud in the language lab. Allow between forty to sixty minutes for this, and get them to write on a topic for which they have already done some preliminary generating of ideas (so as not to come to the task 'cold'). Or use mini-saga writing (see 5.2.5 *Writing a complete text: The mini-saga* (p. 112)), where the limitation on the length of the text makes it possible to complete the composing activity within a class period of fifty minutes. By the end of the session, each student will have produced some kind of written text and a recorded tape of their 'composing aloud' process.

**Follow-up**

Once the students have text and tape, there are various options for follow-up activities. Here are four:

1 Get the students to transcribe their tapes (which will of course take much longer than the actual composing. If time is limited, they could transcribe at least a part of the tape). They read their transcription over, and analyse what they did as they composed, for example:
- asking questions
- planning what to write
- considering ways of organising their ideas
- rehearsing ways to express ideas
- reading back over what they'd written
- assessing what they'd written
- changing, adding to or deleting what they'd written
- checking grammar and spelling

and so on. Have a class discussion to compare notes.

2 Give a questionnaire to the students after the composing aloud session (see *Sample questionnaire* (p. 15)). Compare answers and findings.

3 Get students to work in pairs. They first read their own written draft and indicate in a clear way (textmarker, or red pen) places where they themselves feel that their text is not coherent – in other words, where they find it difficult to follow the progression of ideas. They repeat this with their partner's text, so that each also has the benefit of a reader's comments.

With their own draft texts in front of them, they listen to their 'composing aloud' tape, trying to find clues to their thought processes at the places in the text they have decided are not coherent. They do this either in the language lab again, or (assuming they have access to a tape-recorder) at home.

Finally, they redraft their texts in the light of what they may have discovered. They could exchange these new drafts once again with a partner, and discuss whether the texts still need further amendment (see the two examples below).

4 Get the students to repeat the 'composing aloud' procedure, this time with a text written in their L1. Compare the L1 and L2 writing processes, focusing on areas or parts of the process which they may find easier in one language than the other. Compare findings.

*Examples*

**Liao's transcript**

In the first example, Liao, a Chinese student, finds a way of re-organising what she has written to provide a more coherent structure. She is writing on the topic *Campus life in China*, and starts off writing about campus life in general. Then, as she writes, she suddenly realises that what she is really writing about is the contrast between life on campus as an undergraduate and as a graduate. Here is part of her transcript (the actual words she wrote down as she thought aloud are underlined).

life on campus can be easy, on campus, yes better go back to the life on campus, let's refer to the outline, can be easy and hard, can be easy, don't know what my mum is doing, what time is it? I forgot my watch, where is it? . . . wonder where my watch is . . . OK, ya we have five minutes on this side of the tape . . . if you are an intelligent student, yes and an intelligent would certainly find life on campus easy, or a lazy one, in Chinese we, er, well this, I don't know about the students in our department, get used, it IS easy in our department, for instance, a lazy one can easily, well, escape – it's not like in the schools in the United State that, er, you have to . . . or lazy one, yes, mm, a lazy one, yes . . . . of course you can play truant . . . ya, lazy ones can be intelligent too. I usually play the truant but I don't think I'm stupid . . . but I'm not lazy, but, ya, we did have some lazy students in our department in undergraduate years, yes . . . or a lazy one, as far as, as long as, as long as, as far as, yes, as far as is the correct word, as far as er, all you want to achieve is to pass the exam and graduate because examinations are not, are usually not, are in general never too difficult. So you can have a fairly cozy life if you want to, yes? . . . But it can, it can certainly be hard for for students who either yes for students who either aspire, or aim, ya aim, should be aim too high or . . . too stupid of course, stupid, oh another five minutes, it's probably three minutes, four, . . . mmm similarly would be a right connecting word, similarly the graduate students' life . . . well it's not similar, but in contrast . . . well . . . mm . . . calls for or requires calls for assiduousness assiduousness, intelligence and perseverance . . . mm but this is, well, it's strayed away from my topic, maybe, but I'll change my topic I guess . . . aim too high, in all cases, yes, ya, ya, ya, graduate students' life, well what's the most difficult part in a graduate student's life? well of course thesis, Thesis would be one thing to worry about, would be one thing to worry about, then I'd better put undergraduate life . . . well, ya, I'd better divide it into life of graduate students and undergraduate students, yes, it all depends, depends on personality . . .

**Bao's text and transcript**

In the second example, we see how another Chinese student, Bao, discovered – from the record of what he had actually thought as he was writing – missing links in his written chain of thought. His text and transcript provide us with a very good illustration of what is one of the major difficulties in writing: making sure that what is on the page accurately reflects what was in the mind. In fact, Bao's thought was perfectly coherent; the problem was that he had failed to translate enough of it into written language for the reader to be able to understand it.

First, let us look at an extract from his written text on *The place of tradition in modern China*:

As far as the open-door policy, and being open to the influence of the new technological revolution is concerned, we need large numbers of reformers with the pioneering spirit, who have the daring and the ability to adjust their own production according to whatever the market changes may be, this\* is because of the bondage of tradition . . .

The reader is puzzled in the last line of this extract, because as it stands, the word *this* (\*) seems to refer to the fact that *we need large numbers of reformers*, and the connection between that and the *bondage of tradition* is not clear. However, Bao discovered – from his 'composing aloud' tape – that what he had actually thought at that point was the following:

But we have really few of such kinds of people in modern China. If we speak of the present situation, of course we can't say that there aren't any . . . but . . . why should this be so? Most important is because of the 'doctrine of the mean', the traditional outlook, this is mainly because of the bondage of tradition . . .

Thus, it becomes clear that what he really intended the referent of the word *this* to be was *the reason for there being so few people with the pioneering spirit*, namely, the hold which traditional ideas still have in modern China.

*Sample 'Composing aloud' questionnaire*

Here is a suggestion, based on work by Rosemary Dorie, a teacher in Oxford, for the sorts of questions you could get students to think about after they have completed a composing aloud session.

1 Have you ever done this sort of exercise before?

2 How difficult was it to speak aloud while writing?
   (a) difficult
   (b) neither difficult nor easy
   (c) easy

3 Have you ever thought about what you do when you are composing a piece of writing?

4 What did you think about before you started writing this time?
   (a) the topic
   (b) the length of the text
   (c) the organisation
   (d) the person who would read it
   (e) something else

5 If you have transcribed what you said, or if you have simply listened to your composing tape, do you find that:
   (a) at the beginning, you
      ● spoke a lot
      ● didn't speak at all?

15

(b) during the composing, you
- talked to yourself about doing the activity
- went back and reread what you'd written
- planned what you were going to do next
- talked about the number of words to write
- corrected spelling and punctuation
- changed words and phrases
- rewrote your work completely
- rewrote part of your work
- didn't speak from time to time?

6  What do you think you were doing when not speaking?

7  Does your tape and/or transcript show that you were doing something you were not aware of doing at the time?

8  Were you surprised by anything you found in your tape? If so, what?

9  Do you think it helpful to know what sorts of things you do when you compose a piece of writing?

10  Have your ideas of writing been changed by this experience? If so, how?

# 2

# Generating

*The anxiety there is because buckets carried from the well are time and again empty . . .*

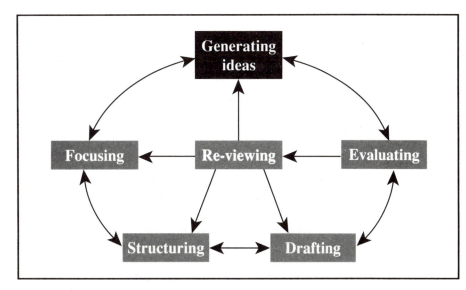

Since writing is primarily about organising information and communicating meaning, generating ideas is clearly a crucial part of the writing process. Because actually getting started is one of the most difficult and inhibiting steps in writing, idea-generating is particularly important as an initiating process. For this reason, the activities which follow can be regarded as belonging to the initial stages, when the writer is still attempting to discover a topic and identify a purpose. Even in later stages, however, idea-generating continues to take place, so that the techniques used to stimulate ideas at an initial stage may still prove useful.

Generating ideas involves drawing upon long-term memory which consists of three main kinds of memory store:

- **Episodic memory**, which is devoted to events, experiences and visual and auditory images
- **Semantic memory**, which is devoted to information, ideas, attitudes and values
- **Unconscious memory**, which includes emotions and feelings

In generating ideas, these different types of memory will be tapped according to the writer's purpose and the kind of writing involved. Thus, the idea-generating process for imaginative writing will be different from that involved in discursive writing. Imaginative writing will tap episodic and unconscious memories as part of the process of creating an imaginary world. Discursive writing, by contrast, will tend to call upon semantic memory in which logically interconnected ideas will be important. Authors of essays, reports, proposals and other day-to-day types of writing will need techniques for getting into the subject and, for the most part, bringing to mind facts and information which can be deployed in a variety of ways according to purpose and audience.

To assist in generating ideas at this initial stage, there are two main kinds of discovery technique: 'guided' and 'unguided'. 'Guided' techniques are those in which a range of prompts – usually questions – is provided to enable writers to discover ideas. The answers which the writer produces are determined by the prompts. 'Unguided' techniques are those in which writers do not rely on external prompts, but generate ideas themselves. Thus, the ideas are not predetermined. Both guided and unguided techniques will be dealt with in this section, beginning with 'brainstorming', which is an example of an unguided procedure.

## 2.1 Brainstorming

Brainstorming is a widely used and effective way of getting ideas flowing. These ideas may be ideas for actual content, or ideas for organising the content. Carried out individually, or better still, among a group of people, brainstorming involves thinking quickly and without inhibition so as to produce as many ideas as possible in a given area or on a given topic or problem. It is an especially fertile means of generating ideas, including unique or unorthodox ones, which can ultimately lead to an interesting piece of writing.

There should be no censorship (other than that dictated by politeness or decency) so as to encourage odd, strange and unusual ideas as well as conventional and more pedestrian ones. In essence, brainstorming should be free-wheeling, unstructured and non-judgemental. Attempts to structure or evaluate ideas during brainstorming can be inhibiting, and will limit the very creativity and productivity which the technique is designed to promote. Judging the quality, relevance, usefulness and practicality of ideas comes after brainstorming, using procedures outlined in 3 *Focusing* (pp. 44–77).

Brainstorming can be used to:
- choose a topic
- identify a reason or purpose for writing
- find an appropriate form in which to write
- develop a topic
- work out a plot
- develop the organisation of ideas.

It is an especially useful technique when writers are faced with a very broad or general topic, such as *Computers* or *The environment* or *Travel*. Such open-endedness represents a problem which brainstorming can help to solve.

If students are completely unfamiliar with the technique, either a demonstration by the teacher (see 2.1.1 *Brainstorming by the teacher* below) or the provision of statement prompts to start them off (see 4.1.2 *Using statement prompts* (p. 83)) may be useful before they embark upon the procedure.

**2.1.1 ▶**
**Brainstorming by the teacher**

Demonstration by the teacher of a technique like brainstorming is an effective way of getting across to students what is involved, especially when the procedure is unfamiliar to them. A demonstration which also involves the students can be even better, and will help to shift the activity out of the teacher's hands into those of the students, which is the ultimate aim in any case. Allow no more than ten minutes for your demonstration. The students' interest will soon be lost if the lesson is dominated by the teacher.

**Procedure**

Before the lesson, make a list of several topics and write these on the board. Alternatively, ask the class to nominate several topics for you to choose from and write these on the board.

1 Brainstorm aloud as you choose a topic, giving reasons and associations which influence the choice you make.
2 Brainstorm aloud ideas for the topic you have finally selected, writing the ideas quickly on an OHT or the board. Explain to students what each idea means to you.
3 Invite students to suggest ideas as well, and add them to those on the board.

*Example*

The topic given to the teacher by his students was *Life in cities*. Here are ideas which were produced during the brainstorming phase by the teacher, who in this particular case used a word processor and video rig. As can be seen, many of the ideas will be meaningless to anyone but the writer. It is only in the later stages, when they are transformed and elaborated, that they will be accessible to a reader other than the author. See 3.1.2 *Loopwriting by the teacher* (p. 47) and 5.1 *Drafting by the teacher* (p. 100) for further work on *Life in cities*, in which many of the ideas generated below are further developed.

crowds
noise
quiet little places
monumental buildings
Luxembourg Gardens
places to visit
restaurants and theatres and museums and galleries
transport: Paris Metro v. London Underground
spaces and places
variety and excitement
cost
need for a centre – Kuala Lumpur v. Florence!
history
convenience: pop down for croissants
inconvenience: traffic jams, chaos
civilisation began with cities

**2.1.2**
**Brainstorming by**
**the students**

Brainstorming is best done in a group, and it therefore both benefits from and contributes to a cooperative approach to learning. By using it, students learn that writers can profit from drawing on other people's ideas as well as their own.

**Materials**

- Slips of paper or small file cards
- Felt-tip pens
- OHP and OHT acetates (optional)

**Procedure**

This is a 'snow-ball' activity, proceeding from **Individual** $\longrightarrow$ **Pair** $\longrightarrow$ **Group** $\longrightarrow$ **Class** with an accumulation of ideas at each stage.

1 Before providing the stimulus topic or question, explain how the activity will proceed: tell the students that they will spend about a minute or so silently writing down ideas by themselves – one idea per slip of paper or card, in legible print – before working in pairs and groups.

2 Issue slips of paper or cards, and then present the stimulus topic or question and write it on the board. The topic can be very general, for example, *Disasters*, or as specific as you wish, for example, *What can be done to improve the kind of aid we give to the victims of natural disasters such as famine, flood or earthquake?* (Cambridge First Certificate Examination 1986).

3 Each student then starts off by writing their ideas on the slips of paper. After a minute or so, they then join with a partner and 'bounce' ideas off one another, adding more slips to their collection. After a few more minutes, get the pairs to join to make fours, and repeat the exchange of old ideas and generation of new ones.

These stages of the activity should take no more than ten minutes, although experience has shown that student involvement and interest can result in twice that time being spent.

4 Ask each group to nominate at least three ideas from their pool. Write these on the board and discuss the ideas with the students so that they are clear about the meaning of each one.

Variations on the above will soon suggest themselves. Class size is an important factor. With a larger class (twenty-five or more students), it is essential to organise students into sub-groups for brainstorming to ensure that all students have a chance to participate. Regardless of class size though, there should be between one and two minutes of silent, individual idea-generating at the outset so that everyone will be able to contribute something to the common pool.

Once ideas have been produced by brainstorming, they can be grouped and organised following procedures suggested in 3 *Focusing* (pp. 44–77) and 4 *Structuring* (pp. 78–98).

*Example*

Here are some ideas produced by an intermediate group of eighteen-year-old Japanese students who were given the topic *A woman's place is in the home*.

---

Brainstorming: A woman's place is in the home

people settles their place suitable for their ability

Every woman should be do homework only.

Women had better do housework.

Nowadays the woman's place is changing little by little

If the house lights turn off whenever you come back home what do you think?

I need husband's help when I work outside.

Many Japanese men think that the women have to stay at home but the men don't have clever reasons.

Almost women in Japan are in their home and make a housework but in foreign countries (the U.S., G. Britain) they have job.

Fathers come back home very late from the company.

A woman is needed to help the child grew up.

If you husband is cook, what do you do?

Most of Japanese women don't work outside. Only in a home, but now that is changing little by little.

---

*Figure 3: Brainstorming ideas for* A woman's place is in the home

A more extensive collection of ideas generated by an advanced group of students on the topic *Smoking* can be found in 3.2.2 *Selecting and rejecting ideas* (*Figure 13* p. 57).

## 2.2 Using questions

Questions, being the basis of socratic dialogue and of problem-solving, are an important prompt for writers. Indeed, one of the skills of a good writer is to think of interesting questions to ask because these yield interesting answers. Seemingly simple questions (*Who? What? Where? When? Why? How?*) can be recombined to form more complex ones, such as:

*How does Who affect What?*
*Why does Who affect What?*
*Why is What affected by Who?*

As with brainstorming, a topic can be given to writers, who then use a series of questions to stimulate thinking, to draw on their experience and to develop and shape their ideas. It is important to realise that, as with any generating procedure, the aim is not to stifle creativity and individualism, but to promote both. Indeed, given the same set of questions, each individual in the class should come up with different answers. Furthermore, as is obvious, given the interactive nature of questions and answers, using questions as part of the writing process can stimulate a lot of valuable discussion and genuine communication among students.

The suggestions which are given here, whilst covering a variety of approaches for stimulating thinking, are not exhaustive. Further reference might be made to the extensive and imaginative range of question-based activities, many used as a starting-point for writing, provided in *The Q Book* (Morgan and Rinvolucri, 1988).

### 2.2.1 Discovering: Using students' questions

Although it is common, as in some forms of guided composition, to give students questions, it is less usual to ask them to make up their own. This activity is intended to start students thinking about the questions to which a reader might want to find answers in the text they produce.

**Procedure**

Between fifteen and thirty minutes can be spent on this activity, depending on the quantity of questions produced and the amount of discussion generated by them.

1 Introduce the topic and ask students to suggest questions people might have about it.

2 Having established an idea of what is wanted, ask students individually to write down at least three questions. Allow a couple of minutes for this.

3 They join with a partner to compare questions and then, after a few minutes, form small groups to exchange ideas.

4 Finally, have each student read out one question. Collect the questions on the board as they do this. They now have a pool of questions to answer and use as the basis for a written text.

*Example 1*

Here are some of the questions produced by a Cambridge First Certificate class in Uruguay in response to the following topic from the 1987 FCE paper: *Describe family celebrations in your country at the New Year, or any other important festival.*

Do economical problems influence the celebration?
Do your family usually meet at Christmas?
Do you think the Uruguayan families give more importance
    to presents they exchanged or to the real meaning of these days?
What do they do to celebrate it?
What about the preparations?
Do you think that the way they do it is influenced by someone?
How many families go to the gathering?
Do your friends participate in the celebration?
What is the traditional food that you eat at New Year's day?
Do you enjoy the celebration?
How many people participate?
Do you receive presents for New Year?
What's the weather like in December in your country?
Do they usually take regards to neighbours like another countries?
Do you think there still remains a religious sense of Christmas Day?
Do you like to go outside in that day or do you like to stay in your house?

Variation 1:
Questions for
sharing
information about
yourself

At the beginning of a course, it is common for teacher and students to get to know one another. It is also useful for the teacher to find out what the students' writing is like by getting them to write something. Thus, a description of oneself is a legitimate and useful topic, while writing for each other has a useful social function.

Invite your students to work on a set of questions they would like you to answer about yourself. Elicit the questions, write them on the board, and tell the students which questions you are prepared to answer and which ones you are not. This is important because of the cultural differences and expectations between teacher and students. For instance, in some cultures, questions of age or income are taboo, while in others there are no such inhibitions. By discussing such issues, a sense of etiquette is established, itself an important aspect of writing.

Add questions of your own which you would like to ask the students, and then have them decide which questions they are prepared to answer, and which they are not. Both you and your students then write answers to the questions as a basis for a text.

*Example 2*

Here is a set of questions based on the above procedure, and the answers which one student gave. A similar set of questions was answered by the teacher.

1   What is your name?
        My name is Abdelkrim.
2   Where are you from?
        from Algeria
3   What did you study at University?
        Biologie

4   What do you hope to study in Britain?
    Biotechnologie
5   Do you know a lot of English?
    quite
6   How old are you?
    23 years
7   For how many years did you study English at school?
    5 years
8   What do you like doing?
    reading, sport
9   What don't you like doing?
    smoking
10   Is this the first time you have come to Britain?
    Yes!

*Example 3*

At a more imaginative level, you might like to try out an idea from Sue Robson, a teacher at a small-town university in China. At her first class meeting with a new group of students, she asked them to write a short self-introduction, using images rather than just plain facts to help her see, hear and experience their world. Here are a few of the responses she received to her questions about the lives of her students:

I was born during the storm of the Cultural Revolution on a hot evening and I came into the world like a wild horse. But now I have been tamed like a sleepish sheep . . .

When the peach blossom came to bloom, I was born . . .

The meaning of my name is 'the silence of the evening' . . .

When the apples in my home town are ripening and the big red apples are picked, I went to university at the foot of the Fragrant Hills . . .

Variation 2:
Questions for
sharing
information about
countries

Getting to know about each other's country, especially in a nationally mixed group, is also a socially useful activity, both for the students and the teacher, particularly at the start of a course.

Ask students to imagine that someone was going to visit their country. What things would that person probably be interested in knowing about? In pairs or threes, have them write a list of questions (which should take about five minutes), and then ask a student from each group to read out their list.

The students then use the questions they have prepared to write a questionnaire to find out what you (or a partner) already know about their country, and what you (or a partner) would be interested in learning about. If they are to write for you, you should collect and answer the questionnaires. If they write for each other, they answer their partner's questionnaire. On the basis of the answers they receive, they can then write a short text about their country.

If you have access to a reference library, this latter part of the activity could be done there, and while you are dealing with their questionnaires, students could be looking up information about their own country for inclusion in the essay that they are going to write for you or for each other.

| Variation 3: Questions for surveys | Questions can be used as the basis for a survey, the results of which are then evaluated, structured and drafted into a written report. (See 3.2.3 *Sifting data* (p. 58) and 4.1.1 *Grouping ideas into frameworks* (p. 79) for further suggestions on processing the data collected). |
|---|---|

Choose a topic according to the students' interests, or have them suggest one. With a partner, the students then think of as many questions as possible on the chosen topic. Stress that they should not at this stage impose any kind of order on the questions, but simply try to make their coverage of the area as comprehensive as possible.

Build up a list of ideas for questions on the board, with the whole class contributing to the pool. Each pair can be asked to contribute in turn until all the ideas are exhausted.

*Either* get the class as a whole to decide on a purpose for a survey they want to carry out, and to evaluate and select from the question pool accordingly; *or*, if there are several possible purposes to which the questions could be put, identify these, and get students in groups to select questions for the different purposes.

Finally, students should think about the best way to present the questions they have chosen and prepare the question schedules to be used in carrying out their surveys.

### 2.2.2 Discovering: Using given sets of questions

In this procedure, students are given questions instead of producing their own as in 2.2.1 *Discovering: Using students' questions*. There is a wide range of types and sets of questions, some of which are conceptually as well as linguistically more demanding than others, so that you may need to make some adaptations according to the level of your students. Also, not all questions are equally appropriate for the topic and purpose of the text concerned. Even so, unusual or incongruous questions can stimulate novel ideas, so that going through sets of questions like those given here may lead to unexpected answers, which in turn can result in an interesting piece of writing.

**Materials**

- Sets of questions on the board, a poster or a handout. Six possible sets of questions you may wish to use or adapt are presented in the following six variations.

**Procedure**

The basic procedure in each of the six variations is the same: present the topic which has been chosen for a writing assignment and get your students to examine it by using the given questions. Encourage discussion and the exchange of ideas in response to the questions, the results of which will provide the raw materials for the text.

Variation 1: Cubing

In this variation, six questions, covering six facets of a topic, are provided. The technique has been called 'cubing' because the topic is looked at from six angles, like the sides of a cube.

*Festivals* is the topic we have used to illustrate the technique in the example here, but you can, of course, substitute any other topic you feel appropriate or interesting for your students. You can also make it as general or specific as you want, for example, *Festivals in your country* or *The most important festival in your country*.

1 **Describe**
What is the colour, size, shape, feel, smell, sound of festivals?

2 **Compare**
What are festivals like or unlike?

3 **Associate**
What do festivals bring to mind? What are festivals similar or dissimilar to?

4 **Analyse**
How are festivals composed? What are festivals part of? What is part of festivals?

5 **Apply**
How can festivals be used? What can be done with festivals?

6 **Argue**
What points can be put for and against festivals?
What reasons are there for taking a position for or against festivals?

Variation 2:
Classical invention

Another way of examining the topic is to use five categories and sets of questions, following the principles of classical invention derived from Aristotle. Again, we have used the topic *Festivals* to illustrate, though variations on these questions could be devised as appropriate for other topics.

1 **Definition**
What are festivals? Classify and divide them into types.

2 **Comparison**
To what extent are festivals like or different from what they are being compared with?

3 **Relationship**
What caused festivals? What effect do festivals have on people?
What comes before festivals? What follows festivals?
What is against festivals?

4 **Circumstances**
What kinds of festivals are possible? What things in festivals are possible? What is not possible?
What are past facts about festivals? What can we predict about festivals for the future?

5 **Testimony**
Where did festivals originate? Who says so?
What statistics are available? What time-tested theories or laws support festivals? What personal experience of festivals do you have?

It is possible, of course, to expand such sets of questions. Here, for instance, is an expanded set of questions for 'Definition':

What is a festival?
  Is it an anniversary, a religious event, a kind of entertainment?
  How many types of festival are there?
  What is a festival related to?
  How are the different types of festival related to each other?

Sets of questions such as these can be allocated to different groups in the class, or to different individuals within a group. The questions can also be grouped by category, thus pre-figuring work on organising ideas presented in 4 *Structuring* (pp. 78–98).

**Variation 3:
The personal
poster**

It is a good idea to ask students to create their own pool of questions which they find useful. These questions can then be made into a poster and kept permanently on display for future reference. Students can also keep a similar record in their workbooks under different headings, for example:

| **Things** | **Animals** | **Events** |
|---|---|---|
| What is X? | What is X? | When did X happen? |
| What is the colour, size, shape, etc., of X? | Is it an animal, a bird, etc.? | What caused X? |
| | How big is it? | |

and so on.

**Variation 4:
The mixed bag of
functions**

An even more extensive selection of questions can be used, covering a large range of functions, not all of which may be appropriate to the topic concerned. Make the questions available on a handout or put them on a poster for permanent display in the classroom, where they can be referred to as needed. The questions are not, of course, in any kind of order and answers will need organising and grouping in subsequent stages.

| **Questions** | | **Function** |
|---|---|---|
| 1 | What does X mean? | Definition |
| 2 | How can X be described? | Description |
| 3 | What are the component parts of X? | Analysis |
| 4 | How is X made or done? | Analysis of process |
| 5 | How should X be made or done? | Recommendation |
| 6 | What is the essential function of X? | Analysis of function |
| 7 | What are the causes of X? | Analysis of origins |
| 8 | What are the consequences of X? | Analysis of outcomes |
| 9 | What are the types of X? | Classification |
| 10 | How does X compare with Y? | Comparison |
| 11 | What is the present status of X? | Evaluation |
| 12 | How can X be interpreted? | Interpretation |
| 13 | What are the facts about X? | Reporting |
| 14 | How did X happen? | Narration |
| 15 | What kind of person is X? | Characterisation |

| | | |
|---|---|---|
| 16 | What is my personal response to X? | Reflection |
| 17 | What is my memory of X? | Reminiscence |
| 18 | What is the value of X? | Evaluation |
| 19 | How can X be summarised? | Summary |
| 20 | What case can be made for or against X? | Argument |

**Variation 5:
The SPRE/R
approach**

An important way of organising ideas, described by Michael Hoey in *On the surface of discourse* (1983), is as follows:

**Situation**
**Problem**
**Response**
**Evaluation/Result**

With variations, this organisation forms the basis of much discursive and academic writing, and a set of questions derived from this sequence makes a useful prompt for writers:

| | |
|---|---|
| **Situation** | What is the present situation? |
| | How did it come about? |
| | What are its characteristics? |
| **Problem** | Is there a problem? |
| | What is it? |
| **Response** | How can the problem be dealt with? |
| | What alternative solutions are there? |
| | What constraints are there on each possible solution? |
| **Evaluation** | Which of the solutions is likely to be the best? |
| | What would be the result of applying any of the solutions? |

If the writer is reporting on past problems and solutions, the questions will be modified accordingly, for example:

What was the situation?
What were its characteristics?
Was there a problem?

and so on.

Such an ordered set of questions defines the basic organisation of ideas, thus providing a framework for structuring the actual writing. The questions can give rise to texts ranging in length from a paragraph to a complete book.

**Variation 6:
The personal
response approach**

Questions can also be used to stimulate the imagination by tapping the episodic and unconscious memory, particularly by drawing on the senses of hearing, sight, smell and touch. Using the senses helps to establish actuality, which is important in developing a sense of place and a credible story. In the following example, Tony Shannon-Little, a teacher in Rome working with a group of advanced students, asked them to write a short story about travelling on the New York subway.

These are the questions Tony used to get ideas going:

---

You are on the street in New York:

   What time of day is it?
   What's the weather like?
   What noises can you hear?

You go down into the subway:

   What is your first reaction?
   What noises can you hear?
   What smells are there?
   What is the atmosphere?

You see a crowd of people:

   How are they moving?
   Where are they going?
   What does the crowd look like?
   How do you react to being in the crowd?

You go down the escalator:

   What are the walls like?
   How do you feel?

You go onto the platform:

   What are the other travellers doing?
   Someone looks at you. With what sort of expression?
   They move towards you. How do they move?
   They speak to you. What do they say?
   What is your reaction?

Your train arrives:

   What do you hear?
   What do you smell?
   How do you feel?

Continue the journey to the destination . . .

---

## 2.2.3 Focusing on what the reader needs to know

One of the things which writers have to consider very carefully, especially when writing for readers whose identity is only partly known, concerns how much writer and reader share in common. Misjudging what knowledge and attitudes the reader shares with the writer can result in a piece of writing which fails to communicate. At worst, it can alienate the reader. Look at the following example:

> Dear Mr Portman
>
> thank very much for your explantion about Civic activities.
>
> (signature)

This writer, a student who had been asked to write a thank-you letter for a conducted tour of Reading Town Hall, did not make explicit certain information which he knew he shared with his reader. By failing to draw attention to this shared information, the writer made it difficult for the reader to comprehend his intended message and purpose. The shared information in this particular case included:

– the day or date of the visit
– the identity of the group for whom the visit was provided
– the role of the writer (in this case as spokesperson for the group).

Another student in the same class came closer to making such assumed, shared knowledge explicit.

> Dear Mr Portman,
>     I take pleasure in informing you that the call at the Civic Centre last week was very useful and interesting for me since I could know many things about the functioning of the local government and some important aspects of Reading and its development.
>
>     Thank you for you attention,
>     Sincerely,
>
> (signature)

Even writers who are at home in the language can forget to make shared knowledge explicit. The reader of the following letter was quite puzzled because the writer had forgotten to specify the place and date of the seminar.

---

Dear Mr White

**Innovations in Teaching and Teacher Education — ODA Funded**

I regret to tell you that this Seminar has been cancelled. Our Representative advises that cancellation is due to the fact that insufficient time now remains to ensure that proceedings would go properly.

I regret any inconvenience that this may have caused you.

Yours sincerely
(signature)

---

It is important to make students aware of the need to consider how much information they have in common with their reader, and how much of what they already know should be made explicit. It is also important for them to realise that from the reader's point of view, a text is more easily comprehensible if the writer begins with what writer and reader share in common before introducing new information.

Some topics may involve things which the students know more about than the teacher. This means that the students really will have something to communicate to their reader (i.e. the teacher). Examples of this can be found in the writing by the Uruguayan students on *New Year* in 2.2.1 *Discovering: Using students' questions* (p. 22), 6.2 *Responding* (p. 124) and 6.3 *Conferencing* (p. 131).

**Materials**

- Four questions, as given below, on board, poster or OHT.

**Procedure**

The procedure outlined here can be applied to virtually any sort of writing, and while useful for idea-generating, it can also be used for selecting and organising ideas (for further work in this area, see 3.3.2 *Clarifying information* (p. 72) and 3.3.3 *Sharing 'expert' knowledge* (p. 74).

1   Decide with your students on the topic and audience of the text to be written. Then put the four questions in tabular form on the board, leaving plenty of space in which to write answers.

| A<br>What do I know about the topic? | B<br>What does my reader already know about the topic? | C<br>What does my reader not know? | D<br>What is my reader's attitude likely to be? |
| --- | --- | --- | --- |

2  Ask students to copy the table, including space to write their answers, and then, working in pairs or small groups, to answer the questions.

3  Write some of these answers on the table on the board, and discuss how close the answers to A and B are, and the differences between the answers to A and C.

4  Use the following questions to decide what information would need to be included in the text:

What is the importance of knowledge or information *shared* between writer and reader (Columns A and B)?

What is the significance of knowledge or information which the reader *doesn't* have but which the writer *does* (Column C)?

*Example*

The topic and audience for a writing task based on the above procedure was as follows:

You are a clerk in the Customer Relations office of a supermarket chain. When eating some biscuits purchased at one of your supermarkets, a customer bit on a hard piece of material which almost broke a tooth. She sent the piece of material with her letter to the Customer Relations Manager, saying how annoyed she was.

The students' task was to write a reply to the customer.

Here is the table (see Step 1 above) with students' completions:

| A<br>What do I know about the topic? | B<br>What does my reader already know about it? | C<br>What does my reader not know? | D<br>What is my reader's attitude likely to be? |
|---|---|---|---|
| Customer bought some biscuits. There was something hard in one of them. | As for A. | What the company will do about it, e.g. apologise, refund her the price | Customer is probably very annoyed. She will expect compensation. |

Here are two questions which arose from the discussion in Step 3 above which focused on organising information in the letter, with suggested answers.

(a) How should we begin the letter?
*Open with the shared information*. That is, refer to the customer's letter and to the problem with the biscuits.

(b) How should we continue?
*Continue with the new information*. That is, apologise and offer a refund. Reassure the customer that it won't happen again.

## 2.3 Making notes

Although making notes on a topic is a long-standing technique, this is no reason to abandon it. Making notes is like using questions: either it is *unstructured*, and students produce notes rather like brainstorming on paper; or else it is *structured*, with headings that are nominated (either by the students or the teacher) to provide a basis for organising ideas when drafting.

Some schemes for note-taking, such as the so-called 'spidergram' (see Framework 1, in 4.1.1 *Grouping ideas into frameworks* (p. 81) and Example 3 on the next page) really amount to an organised display of information which can then be easily converted into a draft. Having a scheme or form of organisation right at the start may help a writer to produce ideas, whereas a completely open-ended approach (as in brainstorming) may offer too much freedom to some students.

As note-taking is primarily concerned with generating ideas and secondly with organising them, correctness and precision of language are not yet important considerations, so use of the red pen should be suppressed at this stage. Nor need you discourage students from using their native language in notes when they are not able to think of the English word or phrase needed. Translation into English can be done later.

### 2.3.1 Making unstructured notes

Tell students to write down individually any ideas that come to mind on the topic concerned, without attempting at this stage to organise them.

As is clear from the example below, not all of the notes will make sense (at least to a reader other than the writer) but this is not important at this early stage. To begin evaluating and sorting the ideas, students can use the procedure outlined in 2.2.3 *Focusing on what the reader needs to know* (p. 30) or they can apply techniques discussed in 3 *Focusing* (pp. 44–77) and 4 *Structuring* (pp. 78–98).

*Example 1*

Here is the first set of notes which a student at elementary level made when given the topic *Shopping*.

things to buy / what kind of things
money
buying somewhere
clothes, books, furniture
the price of the object
the quality
I need something
I have to buy it
I see if I have enough money to buy this thing
I try to see (to search) in which place I can find it
I try to select the shops to see where I can have the cheapest one (quality)
I go to the shop and pay for it

**2.3.2 Making structured notes**

In structured note-making students themselves nominate headings or categories, and then supply information under each heading; or you can suggest the headings. These can subsequently be selected and arranged according to an organising principle for structuring the text itself. In the example below, for instance, one such principle might be *The economic importance of camels*.

*Example 2*

Here is the first set of notes on the topic *Camels* produced by a student who decided to use four headings to get his ideas going.

The use of camels in transport
ship of the desert
best means of desert transport
good memory for route

The importance of camels
a source of water
a source of meat and milk
hair – waterproof – clothes,
    garments and tents
used for cultivation
faeces – fertilizer, fuel

Characteristics of camels
can tolerate arid conditions
don't need food and water
    for a long time
store water in stomach

History of camels
battles
commercial caravans

*Example 3*

In this example, a Spanish student, writing a description of a person he admired, decided to arrange his notes in the form of a 'spidergram'.

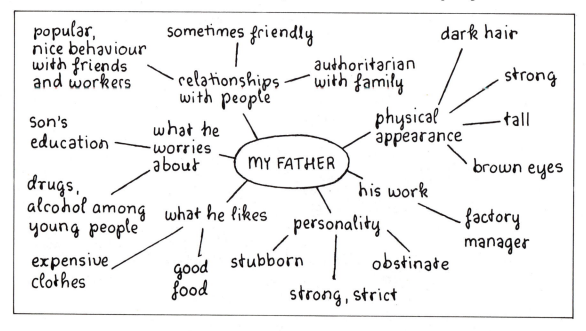

## 2.4  Using visuals

Pictures have long had a role in language teaching (as witness the number of picture composition books) and a wide range of visually-based material can be used in the teaching of writing.

Visual material can be classified as follows:

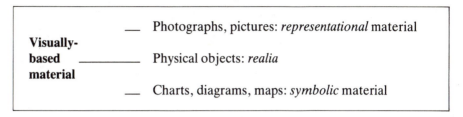

Each type of visual has its own particular characteristics appropriate to different kinds of use. In general, the more detailed and explicit the material, the less room there is for writers to use their imagination. Material which is vague, ambiguous and open to numerous interpretations provides plenty of room for writers to exercise their creativity, and is especially useful for stimulating divergent and original writing within a group.

Realia, including materials like Lego bricks and cuisenaire rods, can also be used as effective prompts for writing. Arrangements of different blocks and rods, for instance, can symbolise real objects, landscapes or even a sequence of events. Writing instructions to assemble or arrange a Lego object or an array of rods can be particularly challenging; moreover, the communicative effectiveness of the text is realistically evaluated when the reader has to make the object or array, using only the information provided by the writer. In such 'write-read-respond' activities, students learn a great deal about how important it is to take account of the fact that in writing, the *text itself* has to carry all the information needed by the reader to comprehend the message.

### 2.4.1  Using single pictures

Single pictures are good as prompts for:

- static or momentary descriptions
- descriptions of spatial relationships
- evoking and describing a mood or feeling
- conjecturing.

The following procedure fosters personal expression and response; even though a single picture may be used as a prompt, each student will bring a different perception and interpretation to it (see *Figures 4–6*). Variations in vocabulary are an important means of achieving such individual response, and if you use pictures for idea-generating, you will probably want to focus on vocabulary enrichment.

**Materials**

- Either have a large picture which can be seen by all of the class, or individual copies of the same picture. (*Figures 4, 5* and *6* are examples of the sorts of pictures you could use.)

*Figure 4*

*Figure 5*

*Figure 6*

**Procedure**

1 Ask students, working individually, to write down as many words as they can based on their response to the picture. (These will probably be adjectives and abstract nouns.) When you judge they are ready, get each student in turn to supply one or more of their words, and write them on the board, until all the ideas are exhausted.

2 Discuss the words on the board. Compare and contrast them and consider distinctions in meaning.

3 Ask students to suggest what kinds of writing they could now develop out of their ideas, what effect they would try to have on their reader and what, as readers, they would want to find in a piece of writing based on the picture concerned. Guide the discussion towards preparing students to start drafting a text based on their interpretation of and reaction to the picture.

Variation:
Using magazines

Bring a selection of pictures to class, or a stack of suitable magazines – the *Observer/Sunday Times/Sunday Telegraph/Independent* magazines are fruitful sources of interesting pictures which are readily available in Britain. Students choose a picture which catches their imagination, and start idea-generating for a piece of writing to be based on it – a descriptive piece, for instance, or a commentary, or a personal response. The considerations in Step 3 above would be particularly important here. If the pictures have already been cut out of their original settings in the magazines, you could ask students to supply a caption, or the headline for an accompanying story.

**2.4.2 Using picture sequences**

As an idea- and vocabulary-generating device, pictures are enormously fruitful. In particular, picture sequences in which there is ambiguity and the opportunity for widely divergent interpretations are an excellent basis for stimulating individual response and a variety of written outcomes. Even at an elementary level, a variety of response is possible, especially if the pictures are used as a stimulus for vocabulary development.

**Materials**

● A sequence of pictures, the content to be related to the interests, sophistication and linguistic level of the students. If the pictures can be blown up so as to be visible in a large group, this will make Step 4 easier to manage (see *Figure 7* below for an example of a picture sequence).

*Figure 7: Picture sequence*

**Procedure**     The procedure below suggests one way of using a picture sequence for a narrative text. With variations, it can be used at virtually any level of linguistic proficiency. Getting students to work in groups during the idea-generating phase has the advantage of enabling them to pool ideas and vocabulary, and this can be a powerful learning device.

1   Organise the class into groups of about five to six students and issue a different picture from the sequence to each group. Don't give any clue as to the place of the pictures in the sequence.

2   Each group should now generate vocabulary for their picture, and then write a few sentences which tell its story.

3   When they have finished, call a representative of each group to the front of the class to display their group's picture. Line the students up in a row, but in random order as far as the pictures are concerned. Ask the other students to suggest an order in which the pictures should go so as to make a story. Note that more than one order may be possible.

4   When the pictures are suitably sequenced, or when everyone is happy that various sequences are possible, ask a representative from each group to read aloud their sentences, beginning with the first picture and the appropriate group.

5   Discuss the improvements which will have to be made to the sentences in order to convert them into a good story. The discussion should reveal that with the first mention of a person, the indefinite article should be used, (e.g. *A girl was walking down the street . . .*) but that in subsequent mentions, the definite article or a pronoun may be used. Note that with an advanced group, discussion can centre on the possibility of actually beginning with the definite article (*The girl was walking down the street . . .*) or even with a pronoun (*She was walking down the street . . .*) as a way of raising questions in the reader's mind: *Which girl? Who is 'she'?* and so on.

**Variation 1:**     Use an illustrated graded reader currently being read by the students.
**Using readers**     Photocopy some of the illustrations, both before and after the point reached by the students in their reading.

Ask the students, working in pairs, to use these as the basis for a story which might include the *events* in the book, but which need not follow the story as it appears in the book. Alternatively, ask students to finish the story beyond the point they have reached in their reading, and subsequently compare their completion with that of the original version.

**Variation 2:**     Take a cartoon sequence of about six frames, blank out the dialogue in the
**Using cartoons**     speech bubbles, and multi-copy the pictures. Either preserve the original order of the pictures or cut them up and scramble the order.

If the pictures are in scrambled order, the first part of the task is for students to restore them to the original order, which tells a story. With the pictures in order, students now prepare the dialogue. They could do this in pairs, role playing the characters.

They then complete the blank speech bubbles and compare their completed versions both with each other's and with the original.

Variation 3:
Using abstract
picture sequences

Use an abstract picture sequence, preferably one which you have drawn yourself (see *Figure 8* for an example of such a sequence).

Tell a story based on the sequence and then invite students to make up one of their own. Highlight differences between versions, pointing out how the abstract style and ambiguities of the pictures give rise to different interpretations. Use the ideas generated as the basis for drafting a story.

An extension of this generating phase would be to have students draw their own abstract picture sets and write a story of fifty to eighty words about them. They then read a partner's story and draw a picture sequence of this story. Finally, they compare reader's and writer's drawings of the same story and discuss how, as drawers, readers and writers, they arrived at their various interpretations.

These stories were written by Polish students within a maximum length of 50 words.

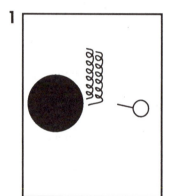

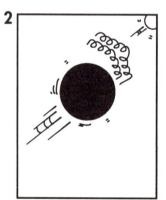

a) Once Small White Prince met Big Black Dragon. The dragon was so big that the prince surrendered. The dragon decided to kill the prince and followed him. The prince escaped for two days until he met three brothers who helped him to get rid of the dragon forever.

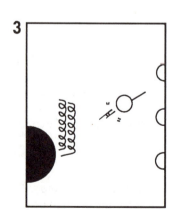

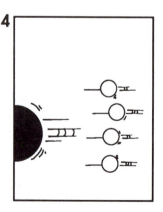

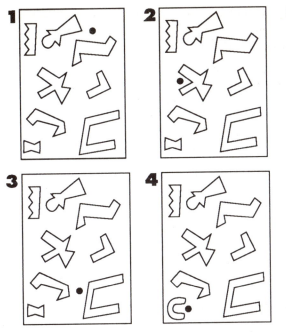

b) One little DX will live in
1000 years. He will be
very alone so he will be
looking for a true friend.
But it will be very
difficult. The world willl
be unfriendly and
indifferent to him. He will
be patient and finally
somebody will accept
him as a friend.

*Figure 8a) and b): Stories based on abstract picture sequences*

### 2.4.3 Completing maps and plans

Incomplete maps and plans provide ample opportunity for creativity, with variation in content and language according to the linguistic level and sophistication of students. You can vary the procedure outlined below according to the needs of your own students.

**Materials**

- Multiple copies of an incomplete map or plan which lacks detailed information, such as topographical features or other elements. Each student should have two identical copies of this map or plan, marked A and B respectively.

**Procedure**

1 Ask students to work with a partner. Each of them should add appropriate details to their copy A of the plan or map, without revealing them to their partner.

2 They now write a description of their completed map or plan A in such a way that a reader would be able to complete a second copy of the original, using only the information in the written description. Use the following questions to guide the discussion about the sort of information they will need to include:

What will your reader already know?
What will your reader need to know?
What information must you tell your reader about at the beginning?
What information will be of most help to your reader?
What information will be of least help to your reader?

Point out that it is also important to organise the description systematically, according to whatever principle of organisation the writer has decided upon, for example:

- a bird's eye view
- a view from the ground
- a view from around the boundary
- a view as a pedestrian walking across the area
- a panoramic view from a central point
- a view from another point or points.

Explain or demonstrate these so that the students understand what is meant. In the discussion, establish the importance of setting up a common frame of reference with your readers, so that they are able to orient themselves in the description as they read it.

3 Ask the students to read their partner's description, and, as they do so, to complete their second copy B of the map/plan. They finally compare these versions with their partner's original map/plan A.

## 2.5 Using role play/simulation

Role play and simulations are widely used techniques in which students assume roles within a context. In role play the students are usually 'themselves' in terms of character, interests, and opinions, but they take on such roles as stranger, traveller, clerk, and so on. In simulations, however, they are sometimes required to assume different personae, as in drama.

Role play and simulations have the advantage of stimulating behaviour, language and ideas in a context other than that of the classroom. For writing, students have a rich source of ideas to draw upon, and since more than one person is involved, there are different viewpoints which can be exploited in a subsequent writing task. Also, role play and simulations can be used as stimuli for many different types of writing.

**Materials**

- You will need to prepare suitable materials for whichever role play or simulation you choose to use (e.g. role cards, instruction sheets and so on). It is a good idea to issue the materials to the students the day before the activity, so that they can think about their roles overnight.

**Procedure**

1 The context for the role play or simulation will probably be based on work already done in class, linked to functional, situational or thematic aspects of the course.

You can either tell students before the role play or simulation that it is to be used as a basis for a piece of writing, or you can delay specifying the writing task till the role play is completed. In the former case, the role play or simulation will be an integral part of the writing task right from the beginning, and will therefore be seen as providing content for an already specified piece of writing. In the latter case, the type and purpose of writing may be derived from the role play or simulation after the event.

2   Organise the class into appropriately sized groups, according to the number of roles. If, in pair work, there is one student left over after the pairs have been organised, give this student the role of observer with one of the pairs. This student can subsequently lead a discussion of the role play or simulation when you begin to consider the ideas which will be used for writing.

3   You will need to give the students some time for preparing their roles, during which you can circulate around the class monitoring, but not intruding.

4   After the role play or simulation has been carried out, have the class discuss the ideas which it has given rise to. If, in Step 1, you specified the type of writing to be done, get students to consider how the role play could provide a basis for the piece of writing concerned. If, however, you did not tell students what they would be writing, ask them to consider the following questions:

What happened in the role play/simulation?
What did people say and do?
What point(s) does this illustrate?
What types of writing could be developed from it?

Since a role play or simulation generates such an open-ended and adaptable range of ideas, you might like to consider using one as a lead-in to the discussion of different text-types (see 3.4.2 *Varying the form* (p. 77)). Ask each group of students to produce a different type of text based on the same input from the role play or simulation.

*Example*

We have found that certain short stories provide a stimulating basis for role plays or simulations which are to be used as idea generators for writing. Somerset Maugham's *The luncheon*, for instance, gave rise to the following selection of texts in one class:

- A short story
- A discussion of eating habits and dieting
- An analysis/comparison of social customs in Britain/student's own country relating to inviting people for meals and paying for them
- The recounting of a personal embarrassing experience in a restaurant/on a date
- A description of an obnoxious/hypocritical person
- A reflection upon the theme, 'You are what you eat'

# 3

# Focusing

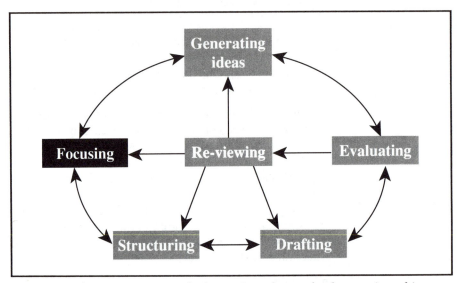

*Set up a word or two to come at the key-points, these to be the warning whip to the whole composition . . .*

When photographers or film-makers frame a small portion of the whole visual scene in front of them, their decisions about what to include in the picture are determined by what they choose as its focal point. And in turn, they choose a certain point as the focus because, through it, they want to convey a visual message.

Writers, too, have statements to make. To communicate their messages effectively they, likewise, 'frame' a portion of all the possibilities for expression available to them by focusing upon a central idea, or upon a viewpoint, which will unify and inform the text they produce. And indeed, a reader's expectation is that a writer will have something to say; that there will be some personal or intellectual commitment to a focal idea or attitude.

This focal idea – or thesis – which the writer wishes to put across is the answer to the reader's question: *What are you trying to tell me?* It can often be summarised in a statement. For example, the writer of an argumentative article might be trying to tell the reader: *My main point is that travel doesn't always broaden the mind*. Or a writer who is describing a jungle trek might respond to the reader's imagined question by saying: *What I am trying to convey is the awesome nature of my encounter with the gorillas*.

Very often, though, this central idea does not start to emerge clearly until the writing is in progress. Elbow's (1973) image of scaffolding effectively conveys what he terms the 'impossible double-bind' of writing:

> 'It is simply a fact that most of the time you can't find the right words till you know exactly what you are saying, but that you can't know exactly what you are saying until you find the right words. The consequence is that you must *start by writing the wrong meanings in the wrong words*, but keep writing till you get to the right meanings in the right words. Only at the end will you know what you are saying . . . You *should* throw lots (of early words and phrases) away, because by the end you'll have a different focus or angle on what you are writing, if not a whole new subject. To keep these earlier words would ruin your final product. It's like scaffolding. There is no shortcut by which you can avoid building it, even though it can't be part of your final building . . .' (pp. 26 and 30)

Something else which readers expect is that writers will have an attitude towards their subject, and that they will make this viewpoint clear. It could be one of approval, disapproval, belief, doubt, support, favour, disfavour. Or it could be a carefully neutral one. Whatever it is, writers need to establish this attitude, because uncertainty confuses the reader, who will be left at a loss as to how to repond to the text. If readers are left with such feelings of uncertainty, the writer will have failed – unless, of course, the intention really was to communicate uncertainty or ambiguity.

The realisation of a focal idea and viewpoint will be related to the writer's engagement with the subject. Its expression will, in turn, be closely connected with the writer's purpose in writing. This, together with other contextual facets of a text (who will read it and what form it will take) moulds the writing as it progresses and evolves into its final shape.

## 3.1 Discovering main ideas

Discovering what it is that one has to say may not come easily. In many cases, writers will only be able to identify the main point *during* the drafting process itself. Indeed, drafting is one possible means of disclosing to oneself a focal idea and a viewpoint, which, as the writing progresses, may turn out to be different from that originally envisioned. Other techniques for finding a thesis such as fastwriting or loopwriting may appeal to some writers, but however it evolves, a clear focus is essential for an effective piece of writing.

The lack of such a focus has two main consequences. Firstly, the writer will find it difficult to organise ideas coherently, since there will be no central idea around which to structure them. Secondly, the reader will find it difficult to grasp what it is the writer is trying to get across, and may react to the text with a variety of negative responses: boredom, disdain, rejection, frustration and even anger or hostility.

### 3.1.1 Fastwriting

Fastwriting is a technique not unlike brainstorming in that it depends on speed and lack of inhibition. However, whereas brainstorming produces lots of individual ideas, fastwriting is concerned with developing and relating them. In fact, fastwriting can follow brainstorming, the writer now developing one or more of the ideas produced during the brainstorming phase. Because speed is important, it is best to have a time limit of between ten and twenty minutes for fastwriting.

**Procedure**

1  Choose a topic. You or the students can decide on one, it can be selected at random from a pool, or students can begin the session with preliminary discussion about identifying a topic, either in small groups or as a whole class activity.

2  Then give fastwriting instructions to the students, along the lines of the instruction sheet below. Note that students work *individually*.

**Fastwriting instruction sheet**

1  Concentrate on ideas, not on language, grammar or punctuation.

2  Write as quickly as you can and *don't stop writing*.

3  Don't stop to cross out or correct mistakes.

4  If you can't think of a word or phrase, either write in your native language, or leave a blank or write 'something'.

5  Return to the blank spaces or words in your native language when you have finished writing, and then, using a dictionary or thesaurus, add or translate the words or phrases concerned.

If this is a new technique for your students, you can demonstrate it first to the class. In this case, the writing can be done on the board or OHP, or on a word processor, with the VDU display visible to the class as a whole (see Introduction p. 9).

*Example*

Here is part of what one student produced using the fastwriting technique, on the topic of *Shopping*.

> When we need something, the best thing to do is to buy it. First of all I think approximately about the price of this object. I see if I have enough money. If I haven't I try to find the (solution) best way to collect the money I need. I (can) try to ask friends or parents about it. I (can) try to sell some other things in order to have enough money for (the object) buying the object I want, or I see in my account if I have the money I need.

**3.1.2**
**Loopwriting**

A development of fastwriting, loopwriting is a recursive process in which the writer produces a stretch of text, summarises it in one sentence, and then uses that sentence to begin a new loop. Each successive loop will help to reveal the idea which is most significant for the writer, and each successive summary sentence will draw upon the ideas developed in previous loops. This process is carried out several times or until the writer is satisfied that the successive summarising after each loop has revealed the central thesis to be developed in the draft. The draft itself will draw upon the content and ideas produced during the loopwriting.

Variation 1: ▶
Loopwriting by the
teacher

Since loopwriting will be an unfamiliar technique to most students, a demonstration helps them to understand what is required.

**Materials**

● OHT and OHP, or word processor with video display.

**Procedure**

Spend no more than fifteen minutes on demonstrating what loopwriting is, because the main point is to have the students try the procedure for themselves. Student loopwriting should occupy the rest of the class period.

1  Talk about what you are doing as you compose.

2  When you are satisfied that you have identified the central idea of what you want to write about, stop and review the procedure with the class. Point out how successive loops and summarising help to focus ideas and enable the writer to discover the main thesis. Note, too, how the pieces of writing are rough and unfinished. They are essentially *writer*-based rather than *reader*-based text. The next stage will be to use the central idea/thesis to convert the accumulated ideas into a piece of writing of interest to a potential reader. (See 5.1 *Drafting by the teacher* (p. 100) for the way in which the writer of the example given here completed the first draft of the essay *Life in cities*.)

*Example*

The loopwriting at the top of the next page was done by the teacher on a word processor and the ideas are based on the notes previously prepared in 2.1.1 *Brainstorming by the teacher* (p. 19).

Variation 2:
Loopwriting by
students

Loopwriting, because it does not demand correctness, helps students to get into the subject and to produce ideas in a relatively uninhibited way. It also familiarises them with drafting as a means of discovering a thesis. The content they develop in the successive loops will subsequently be incorporated into the text in the drafting stage which will normally follow loopwriting. (See 5 *Drafting* (pp. 99–115)).

**Procedure**

Students, working individually, write as quickly as possible on their topic for either five minutes or up to ten lines, following exactly the same procedure as outlined above in *Variation 1*.

---

**Life in cities**

Cities are noisy places, full of hustle and bustle and people and noise and pollution. But they are places which contain quiet places, too. Even in a big city like London or Paris there are parks and little gardens and small side streets which are quiet. **(1st loop)**

**Summary sentence**

*There is a contrast in cities between noise and quiet.* Cities contain monuments, museums and places of importance. There are usually important buildings and institutions, like parliament or the heads of ministries and banks. Cities are where people of power and consequence gather. So cities cater to their needs. There will always be good theatre and restaurants and other places to visit. **(2nd loop)**

**Summary sentence**

*Cities are places of contrast and the concentration of power.* Rulers and their supporters gathered in cities. Civilisation began with cities. And as civilisation evolved, cities developed. Cities becames places where people of power gathered, and round them people of talent and imagination. So all great cities became centres of artistic and architectural achievement. We go to Athens to admire the Parthenon, to Florence to visit the palaces and galleries and to Paris to see the splendid buildings, the broad boulevards, the great collections of works of art. **(3rd loop)**

**Summary of main idea/thesis**

*Cities are the most significant expression of human civilisation.*

---

**3.1.3 ▶**
**Loopwriting and conferencing**

Conferencing is a process of consultation between the writer and the teacher or fellow students. Described in more detail in 6.3 *Conferencing* (p. 131), it helps to bring ideas out into the open because the writer has to explain them to the listener. It can thus be a useful way of focusing the ideas being developed in loopwriting.

**Procedure**

**Alternative A**: Students work individually, then in contact with the teacher.

Ask students, working individually, to do some loopwriting. Then ask them to say what they have written about. You, as reader, give back the ideas to the students, if possible in a form which summarises them, or in the form of a question which leads the students to identify for themselves the main point of what they have written.

**Alternative B**: Students work individually, then in pairs or groups.

After having done individual loopwriting, students work in pairs or small groups and tell each other about what they have written, asking each other for clarification or summary. The discussion should enable each writer to identify the main point they have been working towards in the summarising they have done in their loopwriting.

Point out that by now the students will have a) produced lots of ideas in the drafting they have done, and b) identified the main point that they will want to communicate to their reader. They may also have identified a purpose for the text they are going to develop from these ideas. If they haven't, you could go on to one of the activities suggested in 3.2 *Considering purpose* (below). If they have, they can proceed to structuring and drafting activities.

## 3.2  Considering purpose

In the world outside the classroom, people who choose to commit their thoughts to written language usually have a compelling purpose for doing so – whether it be to entertain, to provoke thought and reflection, to provide a record of events or experiences, to inform, to influence opinion or to request information, and so on.

The purpose of writing which is produced in a school or institutional setting, however, is unfortunately sometimes little more than to exercise or demonstrate certain language skills, or – in some EFL contexts – to reinforce the learning of the language itself.

Understanding the importance of 'purpose' in writing is an essential part of the writing process, since this is what guides writers in making choices about the content they should include and how they should express it. Part of our responsibility as teachers of writing is to make our students aware of the central role of a writer's purpose, and to assign writing tasks where the purpose is relevant and useful in terms of our students' needs and interests.

**3.2.1** ○
**Detecting writers' reasons for writing**

People who write letters to newspapers have varying reasons for doing so, but one common factor is the strength of feeling which compels them to put pen to paper. It is therefore usually quite easy to detect the purpose of letters to newspapers, and this, together with their relative brevity and accessibility, makes them a useful starting point for considering the importance of purpose in writing.

**Materials**

- Multiple copies of one sample letter for class discussion (see *Figure 10*).
- A pool of suitable newspaper letters, either on the same topic or a random selection. You will need to number or label them clearly for purposes of discussion (see *Figure 11*).
- Tasksheets (see *Figure 9*).

**Procedure**

1  First of all, get the class to suggest as many reasons as they can think of why people write letters to newspapers – to complain, praise, thank, correct, put the record straight, oppose, agree, disagree, put an alternative viewpoint, persuade, dissuade, entertain, get themselves into print and so on. Then ask them to have a look at a sample letter, and discuss with them the writer's purpose. Evaluate together how well the ideas and language chosen by the writer serve the purpose (see Example 1). Bearing in mind that the sophistication of the analysis here will vary with the level of the students concerned, a list of questions such as the following could be compiled first on the board to guide the discussion:

What point is the writer trying to make?
Is this point clear?
Is the writer's attitude clear?
What is it?

49

Do we, as readers, need more or less information than the writer has given us to understand the message?

Has the writer used any special language devices to convey the message (e.g. emotive words; emphatic or moderating expressions; modal verbs; juxtaposition of words, concepts or ideas; rhetorical questions; irony)?

2 Then ask the students, in small groups, to work through the pool of letters you have prepared (see the chain of correspondence on the subject of 'noisy neighbours' in *Figure 11*), repeating the procedures outlined in Step 1. Provide tasksheets along the lines of that in *Figure 9* below for this stage of the activity, if you feel this is necessary.

3 Ask the students to rank the letters according to the degree of success they feel the writer had in achieving his or her purpose.

4 Finally, get the class to compare opinions and discuss why they judged the letters as they did.

| Letter | Writer's purpose? | Writer's attitude? | Special language devices? | How effective is the letter (very/ moderately/not very effective)? |
|---|---|---|---|---|
| A | | | | |
| B | | | | |
| C | | | | |

*Figure 9: 'Reasons for writing' tasksheet*

*Example 1*

Here is a magazine article and a reader's response to it to illustrate the type of letter which would be useful for starting off the discussion, as the purpose of the writer is both clear, and forcefully expressed (see Step 1).

# Churning out freaks
## *Mini-cows*

'WHAT is two feet tall, gives a gallon of milk a day and moos?' The answer: the Mexican mini-cow, heralded by some as a pioneer 'in a potential agricultural revolution'.

The tiny animal is the result of more than five generations of selective breeding — which began with the six-foot tall, 2,000 pound Indo-Brazilian zebu. The mini cow produces three to four litres of milk a day — compared with six litres produced by a full-sized zebu —

and survives on a tenth the grassland. Some agricultural experts view the cattle primarily as a protein source for rural families who have little grazing land and cannot afford bought milk and meat.

But others are more sceptical. They question just how long a freak cow, which so disproportionably produces huge quanties of milk, can be expected to live and how

sickly it will be. The quality of the milk is also questionable. How much more sensible to redistribute the land more fairly so that poor families can keep normal, healthy-sized cows. But that, it appears, would be a far more monstrous solution than anything that can be dreamed up in a laboratory.

**Information from World Development Forum**

---

## Cow freaks

I was appalled at the *Update* on 'mini-cows' (NI180). Have scientists nothing better to do than develop such freaks? Don't they know that the ideal 'mini-cow' already exists? Living on rubbish, producing more nutritious milk than a cow, and less susceptible to disease, this 'mini-cow' inhabits many third world countries. It's called the goat.

**Jacqueline Nebel**
**Brussels, Belgium**

*Figure 10: Sample letter for class discussion*

Here are some suggestions for answers to the questions on the tasksheet in *Figure 9*:

**Writer's purpose?**  i) to protest at waste of scientific resources
ii) to suggest a more rational alternative to a 'mini-cow'

**Writer's attitude?**
- disgust
- anger
- intense disapproval
- sarcasm

**Language devices?**
- emotive words (*appalled*, *freak*)
- rhetorical questions to express sarcastic attitude (see sentences 2 and 3)
- contrast of last two sentences to make the point effectively

Sentence 4: long, complex structure, abnormal information order

Sentence 5: short, simple structure, normal information order

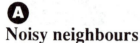

## Noisy neighbours

Dear Sir,
The new occupants of the adjoining house frequently play loud thudding music until late at night. Polite requests to them to reduce the volume have been met with hostility and rudeness. How does one handle a situation like this? Do your readers have any suggestions?
Yours faithfully,
CAROLE MAINSTONE
*London, N3*

## How to cope with noisy neighbours

Dear Sir,
Your correspondent (letter, 8 March) has two options for action over noisy neighbours once friendly persuasion has failed. First, contact the local environmental health department. If they agree that the noise constitutes a nuisance, they should take action, at first informally, and ultimately under section 58 of the Control of Pollution Act. If this is ineffective, the second option is to take private legal action; this could be expensive, and advice should be sought.

Noise is one of the most all pervading environmental problems in the UK, and neighbour noise tops the list of complaints. Research shows amplified music, barking dogs, domestic sounds and DIY activities to be the worst offenders. However, the response of local authorities to complaints from householders varies widely. Some have a clear policy on neighbour noise and provide helpful advice; others appear to be failing in their legal obligation to investigate and act on noise complaints. This society has a neighbour-noise working group which this month is undertaking a survey of environmental health departments. We hope to establish the minimum response to noise complaints, and to recommend methods of dealing with particular problems.
Yours faithfully,
TIM BROWN
*National Society for Clean Air*
*Brighton*
*8 March*

## Dear Sir,

We once lived in a flat beneath the Bee Gees pop group. The only solution to noisy neighbours (8 March) is to move - and quickly.
Yours faithfully,
ANNE ANDERSON
*London, N1*

## Pet hate

Dear Sir,
At least those with noisy neighbours (8 and 10 March) have a legal remedy. What do we do about a neighbour's cats which foul all over our garden, particularly the lawn, on a daily basis? Owners are not legally responsible for their cats' actions and complaints have proved fruitless. Repellants are mostly too dangerous to use with young children about. We might as well be living in a high-rise flat for all the pleasure we can have from our own garden.
Yours faithfully,
JULIA PLUMPTRE
*Faversham, Kent*
*10 March*

## Dogged defence

Dear Sir,
Julia Plumptre's problems with her neighbour's cats are not insoluble (letter, 13 March). May I suggest that she gets a dog?
Yours faithfully,
ANNABELLE ELLETSON
*Abergavenny,*
*Gwent*
*13 March*

## Catty tactics

Dear Sir,
To help Julia Plumptre and her cat problem (letter, 13 March), may we suggest that she acquires a cat of her own who will drive other people's cats from her garden and will attend to its own affairs in their gardens.
Yours sincerely,
LEWIS JUKES
GRACE JUKES
*Bromley, Kent*
*13 March*

Dear Sir,
Neighbours' cats? A water pistol.
Yours sincerely,
The Rev RONALD H. DARROCH
*Stourbridge,*
*West Midlands*
*13 March*

**H**

## Cat calls

Dear Sir,
Perhaps one method to prevent invasion of our gardens by neighbours' cats (letters, 13 March) would be to create a lot of noise.
Yours faithfully,
ANDREW HISCOX
*Lancaster*
*Lancashire*
*13 March*

*Figure 11: Pool of newspaper letters (see page 50)*

| Variation 1: Writing a letter to a newspaper | Having discussed other people's letters, students can be encouraged to produce their own. You could use a stimulus text on a controversial issue, or a recent controversial TV programme, or a current issue in the news as a starting point for discussion of views and opinions. Or (depending on the level of your students) you may like to bring to class a selection of newspapers and get the students to look through the 'Letters to the Editor' pages to find a letter they could respond to. |
|---|---|

Get each pair of students to draft a letter and then to join with another pair, exchange drafts and evaluate them as in Step 2.

After re-drafting in the light of these comments and suggestions, and with a final check, perhaps, from you, the students could send their letters to the newspaper. Alternatively, the letters could be collected and published on a large poster in the classroom, or they could be considered for inclusion in a class magazine.

| Variation 2: Same event, different angle | Taking a single event/situation/issue and looking at how it has been reported from a variety of angles is another way of highlighting the central role of purpose in writing. Choose a controversial issue or event on which students are likely to have differing views. Disasters (such as the Chernobyl nuclear power plant explosion or the Lockerbie air disaster) are a good source of material, giving rise to a suitably rich cross-section of articles: eye-witness accounts, assessments of immediate/potential environmental damage, descriptions of devastation, discussion of causes, apportioning of blame, arguments for and against certain measures, and so on. |
|---|---|

Collect a selection of texts on the subject chosen, or perhaps get the students to find suitable articles from a selection of magazines and newspapers as a reading assignment. The articles should be clearly numbered or labelled for ease of reference later.

Get the students to work in small groups, reading through the texts in turn. Questions to guide their reading could be discussed beforehand and put on the board:

What is the focal (central) idea in this text?
What information does the writer highlight, or make prominent?
How is this information made prominent? (Where does it appear in the text?
    How much space is given to it? Does the writer use emphatic structures?
    Does the writer choose words with powerful emotive associations?)

You could provide tasksheets (see *Figure 12*) for them to make notes as they read, and to provide the basis for a later whole class discussion.

Use the reading and discussion sessions as a lead-in to a writing assignment, where students use the information and ideas they have been considering as a basis for their own text on the subject concerned. Make it clear that the focus of the activity is on choosing ideas and information (and adding their own, of course) which will serve the purpose they want for their text.

| Text | Focal idea? | Which information is made prominent? | How is this information made prominent? |
|------|-------------|-------------------------------------|-----------------------------------------|
| A | | | |
| B | | | |
| C | | | |

*Figure 12: 'Focal idea' tasksheet*

**Variation 3: Eyewitness accounts**

Another idea is to take a single event or situation and consider it from the points of view of the various people involved. Ask each pair/small group of students to choose one of these 'characters' and think about which aspects of the event in question would be important to that person. Ask them to draft a report of the event from their character's standpoint, thinking especially about the reasons that person might have for wanting to give their account of the experience.

One group of students* used a BBC *Crimewatch* programme as the stimulus for this activity. They first watched the programme and discussed the

* These were students taught by Charlie Hadfield at the South Devon College of Arts and Technology, in Torquay.

events and people involved in one of the crimes reported (a bank robbery). Later they wrote accounts of what happened in the personae of various characters (the robbers, the bank clerks, the customers, the police, the bank manager and so on).

### 3.2.2 Selecting and rejecting ideas

Students frequently embark upon writing assignments with the fear that they haven't enough ideas to write about. In fact, once they have set the generating processes in motion, they are quite likely to find that the opposite is the case: there is too much information for the text they have in mind and some of it turns out to be superfluous to their purpose. Selecting useful ideas and rejecting irrelevant ones is therefore an important part of the writing process. In this activity, students work with a 'bank' of ideas created in a previous generating session, and the focus is on deciding which ideas will be useful for the text to be written.

**Materials**

● A 'bank' of ideas collected from a previous session (see activities in 2 *Generating* p. 17). They can be written on cards, slips of paper, OHTs or handout sheets (see *Figure 13*).

**Procedure**

1  Have the students, in small groups, think about a variety of different texts which could be developed from the information they have generated. They should specify a *purpose* for each text.

    A group of students in Cyprus, for example, had produced ideas on the topic *Smoking* which were collected (in completely random order) onto a handout sheet and numbered for reference (see *Figure 13*). Working with this sheet, the students discussed purposes for texts to be developed from these ideas. They also thought about suitable forms for the texts, and possible audiences. They came up with the following suggestions:

A. To complain about Cyprus's bad record on smoking:
a formal letter to a local MP

B. To analyse the present situation in Cyprus:
a report for an international conference on smoking

C. To investigate reasons for people smoking:
a newspaper article

D. To persuade young people about the dangers of smoking:
a pamphlet to be distributed to youth clubs

E. To offer advice on ways of giving up smoking:
a leaflet for display in a doctor's surgery

F. To suggest action for an anti-smoking campaign:
an editorial in a local newspaper

2  Pool the suggestions made in Step 1 above and ask each group to choose

one of the potential texts to work on. They then compile a list of ideas from the 'bank'.

Here, for instance, are the ideas chosen from the handout sheet on *Smoking* (*Figure 13*) by the group of Cypriot students who worked on the formal letter to a local MP complaining about Cyprus's bad record on smoking (Text A above).

7: I know it's harmful but who cares?

10: A good source of money for the government

11: Sooner or later it will be banned

12: It causes lung cancer

25: Economy is one aspect

27: Why should other people be passive smokers?

28: Anti-social behaviour

33: Education – anti-smoking campaign

34: Should be banned in public places

35: Don't smoke near children

36: Pollution of environment

37: Pregnant women shouldn't smoke

40: Unfair to non-smokers

41: Passive smoking

42: Places to buy cigarettes should be limited

43: Smoking should only be allowed in one's home

48: Children shouldn't be allowed to buy cigarettes

65: Young people – enough propaganda?

66: Attitudes in other countries?

70: A curse

78: Waste of time

79: Absorbs vast amounts of money in use and ads

80: Public should react against it instantly

81: Production of cigarettes should be banned

88: Society needs to take active role to stop it

89: Stricter fines should be imposed

92: New legislation needed to control smoking

93: Daily broadcasts of anti-smoking ads

3  When they have selected the ideas they consider most useful for their purpose (and have added any others they may think of whilst doing so), have the groups report back to the class to compare the selections they have made.

Discuss the reasons for inclusion/exclusion of information and ideas where there are any controversial choices. Point out that, as they start work on the actual drafting of their text, they may well find that they will want to amend their original list of ideas, adding some and deleting others. They will also find that the process of drafting itself generates new ideas.

Variation:
Guessing the
purpose

To add an element of interest, you could get each group to decide on a purpose (and a potential text) without telling the other groups what this is. When each group has selected the ideas from the 'bank' which they think useful for their text, they exchange lists with another group, which then has to decide what purpose their partner group had in mind when they made their selection. The two groups compare findings.

1: Smoking is dangerous
2: Only humans smoke – why?
3: It shows lack of willpower
4: Smoking may even harm your children's health
5: Should be non-smoking compartments on trains
6: It takes strong will to kick habit
7: I know it's harmful but who cares?
8: A nuisance for others
9: Mention just one good thing about smoking
10: A good source of money for the government
11: Sooner or later it will be banned
12: It causes lung cancer
13: I can't think of giving it up
14: An expensive habit
15: Enjoy smoking – but what then?
16: Don't smoke in crowded places
17: Disastrous effects on health
18: Most people hate it
19: I love smoking
20: Bad habit
21: Dirty teeth, dirty fingers
22: Unhealthy
23: It has a bad smell
24: Heart attack
25: Economy is one aspect
26: It costs a lot of money
27: Why should other people be passive smokers?
28: Anti-social behaviour
29: Does it show independence?
30: Begins an effort to show maturity
31: Socialisation
32: Shows insecurity
33: Education – anti-smoking campaign
34: Should be banned in public places
35: Don't smoke near children
36: Pollution of environment
37: Pregnant women shouldn't smoke
38: Smokers can relax by having a cigarette
39: Smokers can spend their money how they like
40: Unfair to non-smokers
41: Passive smoking
42: Places to buy cigarettes should be limited
43: Smoking should only be allowed in one's home
44: Respiratory problems
45: If can't stop smoking, smoke less
46: Considerable percentage of smokers have stopped
47: Smokers are not 'in' any more
48: Children shouldn't be allowed to buy cigarettes
49: Youngsters imitate adults smoking
50: Cigarette ends cause forest fires
51: I hate smoking
52: No TV advertising
53: No smoking in a bus
54: Smokers are jealous of non-smokers
55: Some people smoke a lot
56: Boredom
57: People who got used to it can't stop easily
58: My husband has been smoking since 13
59: Smoking is awful
60: Smoking is disastrous
61: Image
62: Low self-esteem
63: Why do people smoke?
64: Women smoke more than men?
65: Young people – enough propaganda?
66: Attitudes in other countries?
67: Smoking sign of weakness
68: Early age
69: A small pleasure
70: A curse
71: It becomes addictive
72: It helps you concentrate
73: Smoking helps you calm down
74: Relaxation
75: Illusion of independence
76: Leftover from unenlightened age
77: Fashionable
78: Waste of time
79: Absorbs vast amounts of money, in use & ads.
80: Public should react against it instantly
81: Production of cigarettes should be banned
82: Life is short: smoking makes it shorter
83: Tobacco industry employs many people
84: Eat fruit instead of smoking
85: Show off in group smoking
86: Smoker has right to smoke
87: Indicates nervousness
88: Society needs to take active role to stop it
89: Stricter fines should be imposed
90: Ads. banned from TV, magazines etc.
91: Do you feel women should not smoke?
92: New legislation needed to control smoking
93: Daily broadcasts of anti-smoking ads.
94: Does it make you feel happy?
95: Does it harm pregnancy?
96: Waste of money
97: Smokers advocate it helps to calm down
98: 2–5 cigarettes a day helps relieve tension
99: Take more exercise
100: Could cause air disasters

*Figure 13: Handout sheet of ideas generated on the topic* **Smoking**

### 3.2.3 Sifting data

We often need to draw upon information and data from sources other than our own knowledge or imagination when we write. But how we use such data depends upon the purpose we have in mind for our own text. Projects culminating in a written paper or documentary based upon research are complex undertakings. And often, although we may have a general intention at the outset, the ultimate purpose underlying our final text may not start to emerge until ideas for the content of the paper have been collected and discussed, or even until drafting is underway.

The principles and procedures in this activity are similar to those in 3.2.2 *Selecting and rejecting ideas* above, the main difference being that the students are starting from source materials rather than simply their own ideas. The focus is on sifting through data and clarifying a 'line' for a text which will be based on information collected from a variety of sources.

**Materials**

- A collection of source materials relevant to a chosen theme from as wide a range of information sources as possible: reference books, newspaper and magazine articles, TV and radio recordings, database sheets, graphs and tables, data collected from interviews and surveys and so on. As this material will take some time to collect, you need to plan for it well in advance of the class. It is a good idea, in any case, to build up files of useful materials on topics of perennial interest and concern which can be used with many different groups of students.

**Procedure**

1 This activity can be as limited or as wide-ranging as you feel appropriate to your students' level and interests, and to the time available. You could, for instance, choose to limit the input to a couple of stimulus articles, such as the two *Tree* texts in *Figures 14* and *15*. These could be discussed with the class to establish a base of language and ideas to work from. Or you might see the activity as part of a much more extensive project to be spread over a longer period, involving more individual reading and research or survey work, with students making notes from the various source materials you (and they) have collected, or interviews they have conducted. Your function in this type of approach would be to monitor progress and give help with language and vocabulary as necessary.

However you decide to set the task in motion, the ultimate aim is to get your students thinking about how they are going to use the information and ideas they have gathered in a written text.

2 After the initial idea/information-gathering stages, get the students to work in small groups, exchanging ideas about different angles which could be developed. Put a list of questions on the board to guide the discussion such as:

Do you want to persuade your reader of a certain viewpoint? If so, what is it?
Do you want to give a positive/optimistic or negative/pessimistic impression of the situation?
Are you going to concentrate on one aspect of the situation? If so, which aspect? Why?

3   Pool suggestions. Ask students to decide on one of them, and then to set about selecting the information they will use for their text. If you want the students to work in groups, suggest that students who have chosen similar angles could work together. They will need to decide which information to include, which to reject, which areas need more clarification or elaboration and whether there are still any gaps to be filled. Warn them that they may well find as they start to develop their texts that their focus changes, and they may want to depart from their original conception. Point out that as long as they are *aware* of what their focus is, it doesn't matter whether it changes. Indeed, such developments and new insights are a natural part of the writing process.

*Example*

The two stimulus *Tree* texts (see *Figures 14* and *15*) were used by a group of students from a variety of national backgrounds.

The students discussed the information in the articles and came up with a variety of purposes for possible texts.

To discuss the importance and significance of trees in their own culture
To compare the way trees are regarded and used in the developed/developing world
To examine the possible consequences of wide-scale deforestation for the global environment
To analyse attitudes towards waste and environmental destruction in their own country

Their final texts were eventually collected and published in a class magazine on environmental issues, undertaken as a long-term class project.

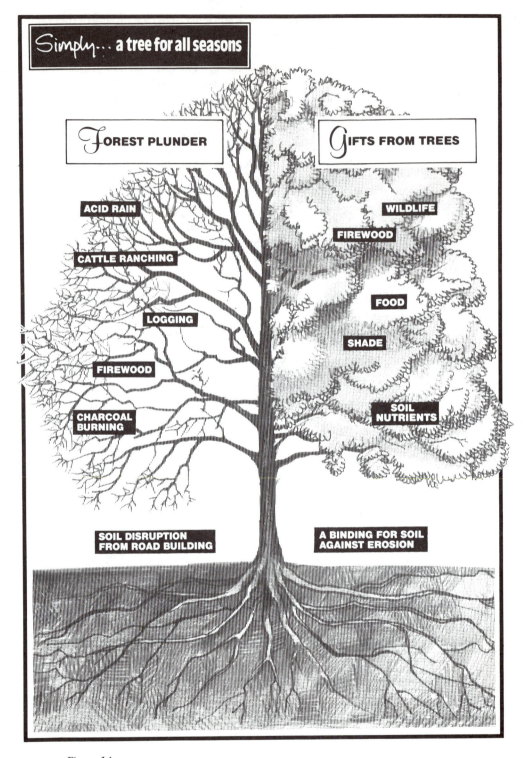

*Figure 14*

# • TREES - THE FACTS •

## Different kinds of trees

• In the colder parts of the world are softwood coniferous forests: pine, spruce, aspens, alders and larches. Often planted commercially for paper pulp, they harbour few plants and wildlife, being dark with infertile needle-carpet floors. They produce acidic soil which make poor farming land.

• Temperate forests are a mixture of conifers and hardwood deciduous trees like oaks, maples and hickories. They are lighter and more diverse than coniferous forests, supporting plants and wildlife. The rotting vegetation produces many nutrients and these generally stay in the soil, which makes good farming land.

• Tropical forests are diverse and include hardwood trees like teak and mahogany. Sometimes 180 million years old, they can shelter up to 100 species of animals and plants in less than two and a half acres. Tropical forest soil is fragile because it is so old and because most nutrients are absorbed by the plant life. It makes poor farming land.

## Death of the earth

**Trees bind the earth with their roots, protecting the soil from erosion and reducing the evaporation of water. When they are cut down the earth is left naked, to be flushed away by rain or dessicated by the sun and attacked by wind. Deforestation is a major factor in the increase of floods. Although it is debatable as to whether or not trees in themselves actually produce rain, droughts have increased dramatically in areas of the world where deforestation is most severe.**

• Until recent times 70% of Sudan was covered by forest or savannah woodland. Many trees were cut down because agriculture expanded, prices for charcoal increased and animal fodder grew scarce. Today much of the country is desert.

• Every year about 15 million acres of land becomes desert, and a further 53 million acres are so degraded that crop production becomes uneconomic. The world-wide rural population affected by serious desertification rose from 57 million people in 1977 to 135 million in 1984. A further 350 million will be suffering by the end of the century.

• In the 1960s drought struck 18.5 million people worldwide every year. By the 1970s that figure had climbed to 24.4 million people annually. Between 1984-1985, drought afflicted some 30 million people in Africa alone. And in India during 1987, 300 million people (40% of the total population) suffered because of drought.

• Selective planting of tree helps reverse desertification by protecting the soil from erosion, improving the local climate and providing for people's needs. Some trees like Eucalyptus use a lot of water and are unsuitable for dry regions.

## Sellers

• More than 70% of all tropical hardwoods are produced by just six countries: Indonesia, Malaysia, Phillipines, Papua New Guinea, Brazil and Ivory Coast. A further eight countries bring the total to 90% - Colombia, Ecuador, Gabon, Ghana, Nigeria, Costa Rica, Burma and Thailand.

• Tropical timber is one of the leading exports of the Third World. It earns as much as cotton, twice as much as rubber and three times as much as cocoa.

• In 1985, forest products were Burma's second largest export, earning $127 million. The same year, sawn logs and timber made up Malaysia's third largest export bringing in $1,434 million. And timber was Indonesia's third largest export, earning $1,210 million. Forest products were Aotearoa (NZ)'s fourth biggest export, worth $348.4 million.

## Tree death toll

• An area of tropical forest the size of Britain is deforested every year. This is one million acres a week, or 100 acres a minute.

• In 1950, 30% of the earth was covered by tropical forest. By 1975, only 12% was left.

• Today more than 40% of the world's original tropical forests have gone. Latin America has lost 37% of its original tropical forests, Asia 42% and Africa 52%.

• The world is now losing its tropical forests at the rate of 7% a year and the end of the tropical rainforests is in sight.

*Figure 15*

**3.2.4
Transforming
personal
experiences**

One of the most common motives for writing is to share personal experiences. Keeping a journal or diary is one way of recording such experiences, and reflections upon them, for possible future communication to others. However, not all such information is likely to be of interest or value to a reader. It has to be evaluated, selected and 'transformed' for public consumption. Sharing thoughts, feelings and personal reactions to experiences through writing about them entails being aware of one's purpose in doing so, and evaluating them from the reader's perspective.

**Materials**

- Handouts of suitable stimulus texts, if you want to use them (see Step 2 below).

**Procedure**

1 The 'ingredients' for this task are notes which the students have made in a personal journal or diary over a specified period of time. You should decide how long or short you want this period to be – a day, a week, a month, or whatever you feel is appropriate. Make it clear that this journal will not be read by anyone else, but is for the writer only at this stage. (Students can therefore use their native language to make their journal entries, if they prefer).

2 Start the session by discussing why people write about their lives and experiences for other readers. If you wish, you could use one or two appropriate (short) texts to get things going. The 'Life in the day of . . .' series from the *Sunday Times*, or the 'My week' column in the *Independent* would be useful sources. Or an extract from a well-known published diary might be suitable, as in the example below from Samuel Pepys's famous diary (*Figure 16*).

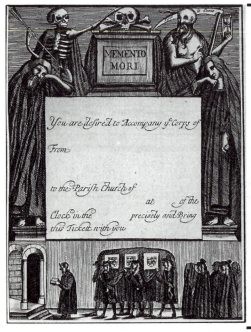

**18 March** ...So to my brother's, and to the church and with the gravemaker chose a place for my brother to lie in, just under my mother's pew. But to see how a man's tombes are at the mercy of such a fellow, that for *6d* he would (as his own words were), 'I will justle them together but I will make room for him' - speaking of the fullness of the middle isle where he was to lie. And that he would for my father's sake do my brother that is dead all the civility he can; which was to disturb other corps that are not quite rotten enough to make room for him. And methought his manner of speaking was very remarkable - as of a thing that now was in his power to do a man a courtesy or not. ...Anon to church, walking out into the street to the Conduict and so across the street, and had a very good company along with the corps. And being come to the grave as above, Dr Pierson, the minister of the parish, did read the service for buriall and so I saw my poor brother laid in the grave; and so all broke up and I and my wife and Madam Turner and her family to my brother's, and by and by fell to a barrell of oysters, cake, and cheese of Mr Honiwoods, with him in his chamber and below - being too merry for so late a sad work; but Lord, to see how the world makes nothing of the memory of a man an hour after he is dead. And endeed, I must blame myself; for though at the sight of him, dead and dying, I had real grief for a while, while he was in my sight, yet presently after and ever since, I have had very little grief for him.

*Figure 16: Pepys's diary*

3   Using the 'spidergram' technique (see 2.3 *Making notes*), talk about the various elements which might be included in an account of a personal experience. It would probably look something like this:

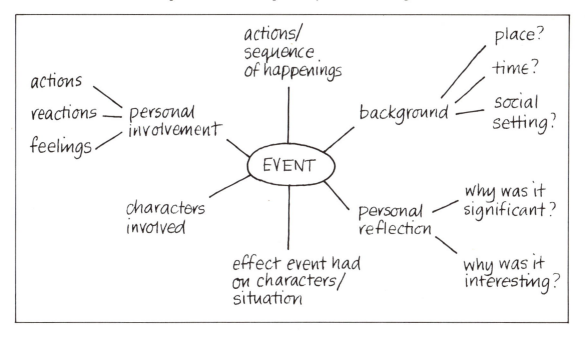

4   Next, ask the students to look over their journal notes and choose an experience which they would like to communicate to the rest of the group. Get them to decide which of the elements in the spidergram will be the most interesting or significant for the text they are going to write about their experience. They will then have a focus around which to arrange the other elements. (Further work on developing a structure for such a text can be found in 4.3 *Variation 1: Recounting a personal anecdote* (p. 94).)

**Note:** You may feel that this is a good opportunity for some 'teacher-fronted' activity, in which you discuss with the students your own journal notes, kept over the same period as theirs. The aim would be to clarify a *purpose* for wanting to communicate your experience, and a *focus* upon which to base the transformation of your personal notes into an interesting account for a reader.

Variation:
Journal exchanges

Another technique based on keeping a journal is an idea developed by Ruth Spack and Cathy Sadow (1983). The aim is to encourage students to become involved and interested in writing by asking them to keep a journal. This will not be assessed or even corrected, but will be read by the teacher, who responds *in writing* with remarks, questions, observations and opinions upon what the student has written. The student, in turn, responds *in writing* to what the teacher has written. Thus the purpose of the journal is a kind of ongoing written exchange of thoughts and ideas based upon the experiences and reflections of reader and writer.

    This technique has been found to be an effective and productive means of arousing interest in writing, which at the same time develops fluency of expression. It also helps students to become aware of *why* they wish to communicate their ideas, and to regard writing not merely as a means of personal expression, but also as a dialogue in written language with the reader.

**3.2.5
Establishing a
viewpoint**

If communication through writing is to take place, writers need to be able to convey their viewpoint to the reader. Their purpose must be to enable the reader to see things from the writer's angle, even if in the end the reader doesn't agree with their viewpoint, or finds it absurd or strange. The following activity provides three variations on establishing a viewpoint: in relation to things, to places and to attitudes.

Variation 1:
Viewpoints on
things

In this activity students are asked to describe pictures of objects and places taken from an unusual angle. Doing this helps to get across the idea that the way we interpret given information will depend upon the angle from which it is presented to us.

**Materials**

- Puzzle pictures of the type which show everyday objects or places from unusual angles (see *Figures 17, 18 and 19*).

**Procedure**

1  Display a picture of an ordinary object or place shown from an unusual angle and ask your students to identify it. Discuss how looking at something from a different angle gives a different viewpoint, extending the discussion to how anything – be it object, place, person or idea – can be viewed from more than one perspective.

2  Divide the class into two teams, A and B, and give a copy of the same list of objects to each team. Team A's task is to write a description of the objects or places from a *conventional* viewpoint, but without mentioning the name of the object; Team B's is to write a description of the objects or places from an *unconventional* viewpoint, again without mentioning the name of the object. If possible, supply Team B with a set of 'unusual angle' pictures to help them write their description.

3  The two teams then attempt to match up the two sets of descriptions.

4  Later, discuss the ease or difficulty with which the matching took place, focusing on viewpoint and the way in which the angle chosen by the writer influenced understanding of the text.
   Also, consider how the unconventional viewpoint, by giving a new 'vision', may have made the description of a conventional object more interesting to the reader. Vivid and effective writing uses such unconventional visions of everyday things and places to arouse the reader's interest and to convey a feeling or attitude about them to the reader.

*Pictures from unusual angles: Figure 17*

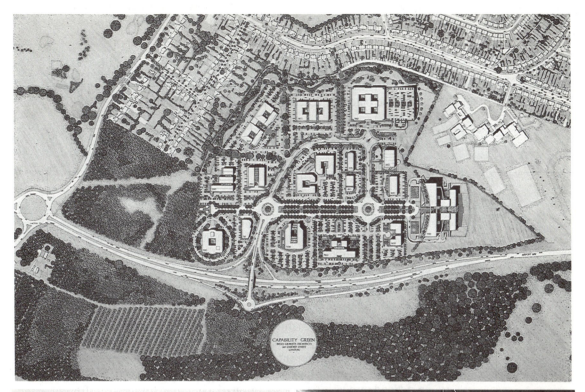

*Figure 18*

*Figure 19*

| | |
|---|---|
| Variation 2:<br>Viewpoints on<br>places | Demonstrating the difference which viewpoint can make to the writer's description and to the reader's interpretation is very effectively done by taking a familiar place and describing it from quite different viewpoints. |
| **Materials** | ● Handouts of a map or plan of a place or a building. |
| **Procedure** | 1 Issue students with a copy of the map or plan and discuss the angles from which the place or building concerned could be viewed: |

● Bird's-eye/from the ground
● From the perimeter in/from the centre out
● Longitudinally/as in a panorama
● Functionally/aesthetically

and so on.

2 Consider which angles or viewpoints would be most useful for different purposes. For instance, someone planning a conference would be interested in a plan of a building from a rather different viewpoint than someone concerned with installing fire alarms. Similarly, a tourist's interests would be different from those of a town planner.

3 Taking the map or plan as the basis for the text, have one half of the class write a description from one viewpoint (e.g. bird's-eye view) and the other from a different viewpoint (e.g. an on-the-ground view of a pedestrian). Then compare the different versions and discuss a) how each description was organised, and b) what features were chosen in each case. This activity could lead into writing a description of a building for use by different occupants (e.g. office workers, cleaners, visitors, people delivering goods, etc.). The same topic can also be used as the basis for some imaginative writing in which students describe the place, building or room from an unusual viewpoint (e.g. that of a fly on the wall, a mouse, a piece of furniture).

| | |
|---|---|
| Variation 3:<br>Establishing an<br>attitude | Establishing a viewpoint is not to be thought of as a discrete writing skill; rather, it should be one of the main considerations whenever students produce texts where the requirements of their reader are paramount (as in most forms of instructions and directions) or where their own feelings and attitudes are a significant part of the message they wish to convey (as in many types of descriptive or discursive writing). Especially important in conveying attitude and viewpoint effectively is the choice of vocabulary, which will be the focus in the following activity. Further suggestions for work in this area are to be found in 7.4.1 *Conveying mood, attitude and feeling* (p. 157). |
| **Materials** | ● You will need handouts or OHTs of texts where the viewpoint is fairly obvious. Choose either published texts such as advertisements and commentary articles from the press, or use examples of students' own descriptive/discursive writing as focus texts. Ideal published texts are advertisements and editorials. With pre-intermediate students, |

advertisements containing a good selection of adjectives will be usable, while for more advanced students, texts dealing with arguments and issues can be used as well.

**Procedure**

1 Display a suitable text (see *Figure 20*) on the OHP, if this is feasible. If not, issue copies of the text, one between two students.

2 Ask your students to read the text silently, to note the relationship between the visual and verbal parts of the text, and then to describe briefly the viewpoint, attitude or feeling it conveys. Write their suggestions on the board.

3 Now get them to find examples of words or phrases in the text that give rise to the theme they have identified. Write some of these on the board and discuss how the use of the words concerned has produced the effects they identified in Step 2 above.

   The theme of the advertisement in *Figure 20* – the accoustic qualities of Pirelli tyres, notably their quietness – is established in the opening caption: *finetuning*. It is then picked up and developed throughout in the following phrases: *perfecting the noise, quietly, noise, a tape of Beethoven, sounded out, sensitive audio equipment, tune it to the least intrusive resonance, putting a Stradivarius up against a fiddle, music to the ears, soundproofing, interior road noise, one decibel, noise they make, another string to his bow*. There are two plays on words – *work in concert with* and *a quartet* (*of his tyres*) – in which each phrase has a musical as well as a practical reference. The theme receives visual support from the illustrations of a tuning fork and of a violin maker inspecting a new fiddle, while the primary function of tyres in providing effective contact between a vehicle and the road surface is referred to in the body of the text: *sets new standards of grip in the most exacting conditions*, and in the terminating line: *gripping stuff*.

   If you are using an OHP, ring or underline the relevant items on the OHT version of the text.

4 If the students are using their own texts, ask them to describe how they discovered what their attitude, viewpoint or theme was and how they were able to develop it as they wrote.

5 Finally, discuss how changes could be made to the text, either to alter the attitude, or to improve the effect which the writer evidently seeks to make on the reader. This will probably involve substituting different vocabulary: adjectives, adverbs, nouns and connectives.

Note that in some discursive or argumentative texts, indicators of attitude will not necessarily be adjectives and adverbs, but modal verbs; the use of verbs like *can, could, may, might, must, ought to* are important linguistic devices for conveying attitude. Likewise, connectives such as *naturally, of course, no doubt, undoubtedly, obviously, clearly* and so on, signal the writer's attitude towards the idea being expressed.

Figure 20: *Text for analysis of viewpoint*

## 3.3 Considering audience

Effective writers are critical readers of what they write. That is, they have to be able to see their texts through someone else's eyes and anticipate places where the message might not be clear, perhaps because they know things which the reader does not; or perhaps because the reader's attitudes and expectations will be different from their own; or perhaps because things which they take for granted will have to be explained to the reader.

The activities in this section aim to get students thinking about various ways in which writers have to tailor what they write to suit the people who will read it (see also 2.2.3 *Focusing on what the reader needs to know* (p. 30)).

**3.3.1** ○
**Reconstructing the reader**

In this sensitising task, students look at texts and try to deduce what sort of audience they were written for. They do this by considering the information included, and the way the writer has manipulated ideas and language.

Depending upon the texts you choose, you could focus on various aspects of the unknown readers: knowledge of the world shared and not shared between them and the writer, for instance; or their possible educational and socio-economic backgrounds; or their probable attitudes and values.

Two fruitful sources of materials for this kind of analysis are:
- *newspapers* which are no longer current (and often, the older the news, the more interesting the reconstruction task). Here the task focus would probably be on the shared and unshared knowledge.
- *advertisements* (with a reasonably high proportion of written text to visuals) or other persuasive texts such as appeals from charities, as in the *Greenpeace* text in *Figure 21*. Here the task focus would probably be on audience background, values and attitudes.

You might decide to cover a range of texts in one session, depending on the level of your students. Or you could concentrate on only one of the areas suggested above.

Variation 1:
Using newspaper texts

**Materials**

- Multiple copies of a text or texts from a newspaper which is no longer current (see *Figure 26*, the texts in 4.2 *Experimenting with arrangements* (p. 90)).
- Text-liners or red pens.

**Procedure**

1 Do not reveal the context of the text(s) you have chosen at this stage. (This may involve deleting the title). Ask your students to read the text, highlighting with a text-liner any information which is not clear to them, or any parts of the text they don't understand because they lack background knowledge.

2 Then ask the students, working in twos or threes, to compare what they have highlighted. The aim is to get down to a core of non-understood information (i.e. if any members of the group do understand something which the others don't, they should explain it). Compile on the board or OHP a list of non-understood items by pooling the results of the above discussions.

3 Now reveal the context of the text, or get students to guess it. Try to eliminate items from the list on the board in the light of this new knowledge.

Invite suggestions as to how the information reported in the text(s) would have to be re-written or glossed for a present-day audience by considering such things as:

- What does the writer assume that we (as readers) know which we actually don't know?
- What extra information is needed?
- Where does it need to be added?

## Variation 2: Using advert texts

**Materials**

- A pool of suitable texts, mounted on strong card or paper (to survive re-use by several groups) and clearly numbered for reference. Have a supply of tasksheets ready (along the lines of that in *Figure 22*) for the students to make notes as they consider the texts.

**Procedure**

1 Ask students, in twos or threes, to consider each text in turn, making notes under the following headings on their tasksheets as they do so:

What audience is the text aimed at?
What is the purpose of the text?
What ideas and persuasive points are used?
Which ideas are most effective?
Which language features help to influence our reactions (as readers) to the text?

Follow this with a whole class discussion to pool opinions and conclusions, each group taking it in turn to introduce one of the texts.

2 As an extension of this activity, you could ask each group to draft an appeal or advertisement of their own. Get them to focus on evaluating their ideas in terms of the audience they have in mind.

After they have drafted their texts, groups can check each other's drafts according to the questions above.

*Example*

The appeal from the environmental organisation Greenpeace (*Figure 21* opposite), is an example of the kind of text we have used successfully for this activity.

# PLANET EARTH IS 4,600 MILLION YEARS OLD

If we condense this inconceivable time-span into an understandable concept, we can liken Earth to a person of 46 years of age.

Nothing is known about the first 7 years of this person's life, and whilst only scattered information exists about the middle span, we know that only at the age of 42 did the Earth begin to flower.

Dinosaurs and the great reptiles did not appear until one year ago, when the planet was 45. Mammals arrived only 8 months ago; in the middle of last week man-like apes evolved into ape-like men, and at the weekend the last ice age enveloped the Earth.

Modern man has been around for 4 hours. During the last hour, Man discovered agriculture. The industrial revolution began a minute ago.

During those sixty seconds of biological time, Modern Man has made a rubbish tip of Paradise.

He has multiplied his numbers to plague proportions, caused the extinction of 500 species of animals, ransacked the planet for fuels and now stands like a brutish infant, gloating over this meteoric rise to ascendancy, on the brink of the final mass extinction, and of effectively destroying this oasis of life in the solar system.

## AGAINST ALL ODDS

GREENPEACE

---

# G R E E N P E A C E

Against all odds, Greenpeace has brought the plight of the natural world to the attention of caring people. Terrible abuses to the environment, often carried out in remote places or far out to sea have been headlined on television and in the press.

Greenpeace began with a protest voyage into a nuclear test zone. The test was disrupted. Today, the site at Amchitka in the Aleutian Islands is a bird sanctuary.

Then Greenpeace sent its tiny inflatable boats to protect the whales. They took up position between the harpoons and the fleeing whales. Today, commercial whaling is banned.

On the ice floes of Newfoundland, Greenpeace volunteers placed their bodies between the gaffs of the seal hunters and the helpless seal pups. The hunt has since been called off.

In the North Atlantic, Greenpeace drove its inflatables underneath falling barrels of radioactive waste. Now nuclear waste dumping at sea has been stopped.

In the North Sea, Greenpeace swimmers

turned back dump ships carrying chemical wastes. New laws to protect the North Sea have been promised.

Peaceful direct action by Greenpeace has invoked the power of public opinion which in turn has forced changes in the law to protect wildlife and to stop the pollution of the natural world.

*Figure 21: 'Analysing audience' text*

Here are the notes one group of students made on their tasksheet:

| Text | 1 |
|------|---|
| Audience | • People who are aware of need for protection of the environment but who are not very strongly committed |
| Purpose | • to draw more attention to human race's destruction of the planet<br>• to persuade more people to join Greenpeace campaign |
| Main ideas in text | • insignificance of human race in comparison with age of planet<br>• condensing of age of universe into an understandable concept<br>• disproportionate destruction caused by human race in their minute on earth<br>• imminent destruction of life on earth<br>• contrast between huge commercial forces of destruction and tiny volunteer Greenpeace forces of salvation |
| Most effective ideas | • metaphor of rubbish tip in contrast with Paradise<br>• time-span analogy |
| Language features | • negative words: *plague, brutish, ransacked, gloating*<br>• emotive words: *plight, abuse, sanctuary, tiny, helpless*<br>• images which suggest analogy of David and Goliath battle |

*Figure 22: 'Analysing audience' tasksheet*

**3.3.2 Clarifying information**

When we write about things we are familiar with, we often tend to underestimate the need to explain them to a reader who is not familiar with them. In this activity, the focus is on clarifying culture-specific or event-specific references. You can use published texts as a starting point for discussion and then move on to getting the students to consider their own draft texts.

**Materials**

• Multiple copies of a few short texts (from current newspapers or magazines) with clear *Anglophone* culture-specific references to such things as food, customs, habits, educational or governmental systems and so on (see *Figure 23*).
• Text-liners or red pens.
• Students' own draft texts – you will need two copies of each student's draft.

**Procedure**

1 Ask your students to work through as many of the published texts as time permits, highlighting information which is not clear to them. As they do this, write up a list of questions on the board such as the following:

Do I understand the subject of the text?
Do I understand who the people involved are?
Are their positions and relations to each other clear?
Is it clear where, when, why and how the events in the text took place?
Do I understand the significance of the events/people/issues in the text?

2   Use these questions as a basis for suggestions from the class as to how they would clarify the information in the text for an audience from their own country. In a multi-national group, draw attention to those aspects of the text which might need more clarification for certain nationalities than for others.

3   Use similar procedures with the students' own draft texts on a topic which is culturally loaded, for example, an account of a custom or festival in their country, or a significant event which took place there recently. (The draft texts on *New Year festivities* by Uruguayan students in 6.2 *Responding* and 6.3 *Conferencing* (pp. 124 and 131) would be the sort of texts to use for this activity).

Ask the students to exchange drafts with a partner and to evaluate each other's work according to the questions in Step 1 above. They should then use the comments of their partner to help them re-draft their texts.

In multi-national groups, try to make sure the partners are from different countries. In single-nationality groups, get students to focus on clarifying each other's texts for a reader who is not familiar with their country.

---

# HORSE AND CAR

*From Mr Ken Pursey*

GORDON WINTER is right to say, in his article '(Bridleways) for safety"(September 1), that we are taking the problem from the wrong angle. Local regulation should prevent further increase in (horse culture) in areas where there is nowhere to exercise or ride horses except on the roads. Certainly, building a rapport between car and horse owners is a good thing, but unless something is done to improve (bridlepaths) and (common land) so that people can exercise in winter as well as summer, giving them a Road Safety Certificate does not make them any safer.

As one who has experienced the loss of a horse on the road I know how hard it is for cars and horses to co-exist. A car running at only 10 miles an hour can cause irreparable damage; flesh and blood can never mix with metal. The powers that be should insist on sanded tracks being made in forestry to take these folk off the roads. Such bodies as the Forestry Commission charge for riding, yet do nothing to make it possible to exercise in winter. If riding tracks are made solely for horses, there would be no need for argument between walkers and their dogs regarding the condition of paths used.

Since moving to this part of Sussex 14 years ago, I have seen horse owners take over surrounding acres, so that there are now 26 horses within a mile.

— KEN PURSEY, *Gatewood, Wilmington, East Sussex.*

*Figure 23: Sample 'culture-specific' text*

### 3.3.3 Sharing 'expert' knowledge

We are often unaware of the extent to which we need to spell out for an audience ideas or concepts which are self-explanatory to us. Trying to explain areas of expertise to non-experts, especially in writing, is an effective way of making this point.

The aim of this activity is to get both 'expert' and 'novice' to be aware of which information is clear, and which needs clarification and/or elaboration on the part of the expert.

**Materials**

- Tape recorders (preferably one per group).
- Text-liners or red pens.

**Procedure**

1  Ask your students to think, before class, of something they know how to do well – a skill they have such as the preparation of a national dish, for example; or more esoteric accomplishments such as bee-keeping or bonsai; or, on a simpler level, how to carry out an everyday transaction in their country, such as making a telephone call from a public call-box. Tell them they have to be prepared to explain their expertise to the others and give instructions to 'novices'.

2  In class, you need to organise students into small groups, each with a tape recorder. Each group chooses one member whose expertise they would like to share. This 'expert' then gives instructions *orally* to the others, who take notes (with the ultimate aim of *writing* a set of instructions). This stage of the task is taped.

3  Meanwhile, write a few questions on the board to guide the discussion in the next stage, in which each group re-plays its tape, asking for clarification where information and procedures are not clear:

Have we got enough information about each stage of the operation to proceed to the next?
Has the expert explained the reasons for telling us to do certain things?
Do we need to understand why we have to do them?

Each group then collectively drafts a written set of instructions. Circulate among the groups, giving help with language where necessary.

4  Each group now exchanges drafts with another group. They should read the instructions they have been given, and highlight anything which is not clear. The 'expert' concerned can then be asked to give further clarification.

Variation: Interviewing an expert

A variation would be to get students to work in small groups (of four or so). One student is chosen to be the 'expert', but instead of giving instructions, they are interviewed by the others about their expertise. The whole interview is recorded.

Groups then exchange tapes, and write a set of instructions using the information on the tape. Finally, each group reads out its instructions to the rest of the class, and if they are not clear, the expert concerned is called upon to give further clarification.

## 3.4 Considering form

Learning to write in a foreign or second language involves much more than acquiring the linguistic tools of words and structures with which to communicate meaning, essential though these are. What is also needed is knowledge about how different kinds of texts are conventionally structured and presented in that language.

As readers, we have certain expectations about the likely content, structure, development and graphic appearance of different types of written texts. These expectations, stored as abstract mental structures (*schemata*) in long-term memory, are used by both writers and readers in composing and reading. It is important, therefore, that the writer matches the reader's expectations in order to facilitate comprehension, unless, of course, a decision is made to convey part of the meaning by deliberately flouting them.

**3.4.1** ○
**Comparing characteristics of text-types**

The focus in this sensitising activity is on the sense of form which prompts good writers to search for the most appropriate way in which to present their ideas. In many EFL/ESL situations, students will already have acquired a certain knowledge of this form from reading and writing in their first language, but they may still need to consider whether the conventions of form differ in English. In other situations, students may need more fundamental work on recognising and assimilating the features typical of different kinds of texts.

**Materials**

- A collection of examples of various types of texts, clearly numbered and mounted on card (to survive re-use by different groups). Obviously, it would be impossible to cover all types of text in such an activity, nor would it be useful to do so. What is needed is a range of texts (suitable for your students' level) in which features of format, layout, style and content contrast clearly with each other, so that students are able to identify the texts as certain types of writing.
- Handouts of one or two of the above texts for whole class discussion.

**Procedure**

1   Have a brief brainstorming session to discover as many types of writing as the students can think of. Then look at the one or two sample texts on the handout. Ask students to identify the types of texts they are, and to analyse them for features such as:

**Format**:                    the way the text is set out on the page

**Organisation**:        the way the text is *segmented* – sections? paragraphs? stanzas? etc.

the way the text is *signposted* – headings? salutations? paragraph indentations? etc.

**Style**:                       the words and structures chosen – formal/informal/ casual? direct/indirect? personal/impersonal? emotive/ dispassionate? use of notes or abbreviations?

and so on.

2   Then get students, in pairs, to work through the other texts from the pool, paying attention to the features discussed above. A tasksheet for making notes would be helpful (such as the analysis chart in *Figure 24*). Later, compare opinions and observations in a whole class discussion.

3   As an on-going project, you could suggest to students that they compile their own text-type file, or perhaps that the class compile a collective file to which students contribute examples of various types of texts.

Variation:  ○
Newspaper scan

One quick way of getting sufficient examples to make the point in this activity is to use a daily newspaper. Have students in small groups and make sure there are enough copies of the newspaper for each group to have its own. Before class, mark a number of contrasting types of texts in the newspapers. Get each student (or pair) in the group to work on a different page of the newspaper, analysing the marked texts (as in Step 1 above). This should ensure that everyone has something to contribute to the subsequent whole class discussion.

| Text | Type of writing | Format | Style | Organisation |
|------|-----------------|--------|-------|--------------|
| 1 | postcard | • address on right<br>• message on left | • personal, informal<br>• abbreviations used<br>• ideas often in note form | • date and place as heading<br>• no indication of addressee<br>• no paragraphs |
| 2 | formal business letter | | | |
| 3 | page from academic article | | | |
| 4 | editorial from newspaper | | | |
| 5 | recipe | | | |
| 6 | telephone message | | | |
| 7 | page from a novel | | | |
| 8 | poem | | | |

*Figure 24: Text-type analysis chart*

**3.4.2 Varying the form**

This activity would best be used as a follow-up to the analysis of text-types suggested in 3.4.1 *Comparing characteristics of text-types*. The idea here is to get students to experiment with using the same basic ideas in a variety of ways for different types of text. It could form the starting point for a series of lessons in which the draft texts produced here provide the raw materials for a variety of 'evaluating' and 're-viewing' tasks (see relevant sections on pp. 116–135 and pp. 136–171 respectively).

**Materials**

● A collection of ideas from a previous generating activity, as open-ended and flexible as possible. The range of ideas which might be generated from an evocative visual stimulus (see 2.4.1 *Using single pictures, Figures 4–6* (p. 36)), or the kind of ideas which might arise from the role play in 2.5 *Using role play/simulation* (p. 42) would be suitable.

**Procedure**

1  Invite the students to think about how they could use the ideas they have generated in different types of texts. One class of students, for instance, who had brainstormed ideas on the topic *Prisons* came up with the following suggestions for texts to be developed from them:

A personal letter from a prisoner
An essay on the effectiveness of imprisonment as a form of punishment
A description of a prison
A poem/word picture
A short story
A newspaper editorial arguing for alternatives to imprisonment
An interview with a prison officer about his job

2  Ask students to draft a text which takes the form of one of the types of writing suggested. They will have to think about which ideas they are going to use, how they will organise their text, how they will set it out on the page, and what sort of language they will choose. Make sure that each type of text is covered.

3  In a subsequent session, pair each student with a partner who has written a different type of text. Ask them to read each other's drafts and discuss the differences in style, organisation and layout. Get them to suggest improvements where appropriate.

4  A nice way to conclude this activity is to group students according to the types of texts they have written. Get them to select the text they think is most successful as a representative of that particular form, polish the drafts, and eventually 'publish' them on a wall-display or in an edition of a class magazine.

# 4

# Structuring

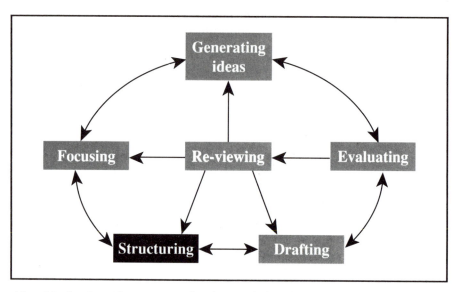

*After this, he chose from among the ideas and placed them in order; he scrutinised the expressions and placed them where they belonged . . .*

Conveying a message through writing is essentially a matter of selecting information – both factual and linguistic – and arranging, or more precisely, structuring it. And since writers are communicating with readers who are distant both in time and space, the decisions they take about what information to select and how to arrange it are crucial to the success – or otherwise – with which the message is conveyed and received.

Structuring information entails various organisational processes of grouping ideas together and deciding upon how to sequence them. However, as we are no doubt aware from our own experience, we very rarely know exactly what we are going to write and how we are going to present it until we actually start writing. Although we may start off with a general organisational scheme, new ideas are constantly generated by the actual process of writing, which means that we continually have to readjust our original plans. In other words, writing should not be thought of as a process where organisation of ideas is a preliminary and finite stage, but rather where on-going *re-organisation* is the keyword.

Most people, however, do find it helpful to group their ideas and impose some sort of order upon them before they start on a first draft, even if they know that the structure of the final text may turn out to be quite different from how they initially conceived it. The problem is, though, that people frequently fail to go beyond this preliminary structuring stage, and a common misconception on the part of students is that organisational schemes and outlines, once learnt, can be rigidly applied to any piece of writing they do: the *Introduction – Paragraph 1 – Paragraph 2 – Paragraph 3 – Conclusion* approach. What such an approach fails to take into account is that each piece of writing is different: it has its own context, and its own rationale.

We believe it is therefore more helpful to approach the structuring of a text by asking questions such as the following:

- Why am I writing? What do I hope to achieve by writing? Do I want to shock? persuade? criticise? entertain? inform?

- In view of my purpose, is there any particularly important, significant or interesting idea which I need to get across?

- Can I see how all my other ideas relate to this key idea?

- How shall I deal with this key idea in my text: start off with this idea? save it for last? lead up to it gradually? re-cycle it in various guises throughout?

- Will the reader expect me to arrange the information in a certain way?

- If so, shall I comply with this expectation, or deviate from it? Which approach will have the greater impact?

## 4.1 Ordering information

The focus in this group of activities is on the initial fitting together of ideas into clusters or categories, so as to impose some kind of preliminary order on an unwieldy collection of data.

**4.1.1 Grouping ideas into frameworks**

Almost every act of writing involves categorising and grouping procedures to a greater or lesser degree, but it is easiest to illustrate them clearly in tasks which demand getting to grips with unstructured masses of information. In this activity, therefore, work with information which students have collected in surveys or interviews (see 2.2.1, *Variation 3: Questions for surveys* (p. 25)), or use describing or classifying tasks, where decisions have to be made about the conceptual relationships between ideas and their hierarchical arrangements.

**Procedure**

1 We assume that the students will be working with previously generated ideas or data. First, get them, in small groups, to think about possible categories or headings under which their information could be arranged. A class of students in China, for instance, used a text reporting a survey of habits amongst British teenagers as a basis for a description of teenagers in their own country.

They decided to group their ideas under the following headings:

How teenagers spend their money
What they do in their spare time
What kind of food they like
Their daily routine
Their attitudes to their parents
Their attitudes to their home
Their attitudes towards school/study

2   The next stage is to get students to discuss how to arrange their groups of ideas/information. You could put questions such as the following on the board to guide the discussion:

Can we rank the categories in order of significance?
If so, which shall we deal with first? Which last?
Is there any category which is particularly important/significant/
    interesting? If so, could this provide a focus for the text?
Are there any categories which contrast significantly with each other? If
    so, could this contrast be used as the basis for organising the information?

3   Ask each group of students to prepare a preliminary framework for their text (on an OHT if feasible). They present it to the rest of the class, explaining why they have decided to group their ideas as they have. If new ideas arise as they do this, get the class to suggest how and where to include them. These frameworks then provide a starting-off point for the first draft.

*Examples*   Here are two examples of frameworks produced for various kinds of texts.

**Framework 1**
The first framework, produced for a classification type of text by a group of students on a pre-sessional course at a British university, uses the so-called 'spidergram' technique for grouping information. The students worked together to produce a range of ideas on the topic of crops, making clear the conceptual relationships between them (see their spidergram in *Figure 25*).
    This kind of visual display has several useful features:
- The hierarchical relationship of ideas becomes immediately obvious (e.g. *legumes* = class; *beans* = member of class)
- Both the generating and the grouping of ideas take place simultaneously, so that the writing process is already well advanced by the time such a diagram is finished.

When the first draft of linear text is produced, students have to focus on choosing language which will provide enough linguistic signposts to transpose effectively into written form the visual clarity of the diagram.

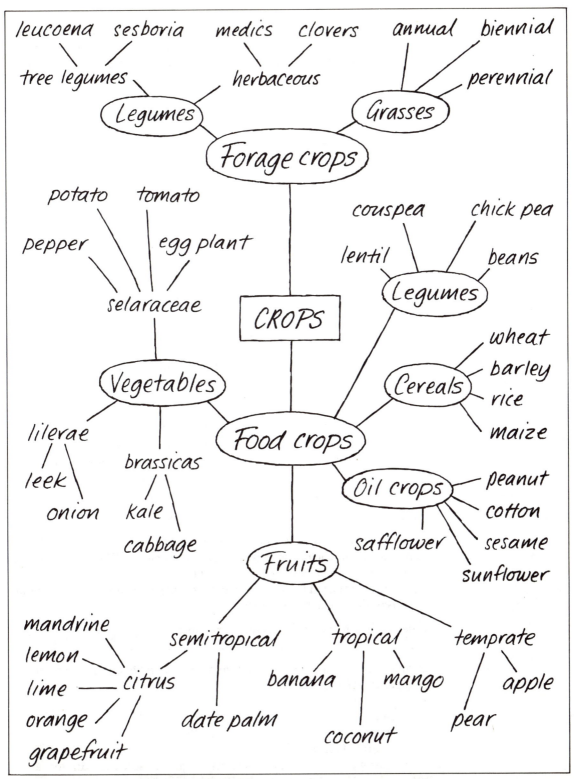

Figure 25: 'Crops' spidergram

**Framework 2**

The second framework was produced by students in Cyprus who were writing a report based on a survey they had carried out on attitudes of Cypriot people towards tourism in their country. Here are the headings under which they first considered their findings:

|  | **Positive points** | **Negative points** |
|---|---|---|
| A: **Traditions** | can learn from tourists about other nations' customs & traditions | tourism changing traditional way of life in Cyprus |
| B: **Ideas** | broadens outlooks | could lead to moral corruption |
| C: **Economic factors** | helps economic development | local people can't enjoy own country – shortage of hotels, prices pushed up<br><br>causes damage to environment<br><br>villages dying because young people seek work in tourist centres |
| D: **Interpersonal relations** | can lead to understanding between different peoples | leads to shortages of husbands for Cypriot women (too many inter-marriages)<br><br>danger of AIDS<br><br>tourist types sometimes not representative of the majority – can lead to misunderstanding |

After further discussion, they came to two conclusions:

(a) Category C above was the most important point; they would deal with it last, and use it to lead into their conclusion: *we face a dilemma, because we need tourism but the present price is too high*.

(b) The most significant finding was that people had very *mixed feelings* about tourism; this would be their focus.

This meant that their second scheme looked like this:

> People's attitudes towards tourism: mixed. Can be seen in how they regard the effects of tourism on:
> A: traditions
> B: ideas           } (details as above
> D: interpersonal relations    in Framework 1)
> C: economic factors
> Concluding point: most people think we are faced with a dilemma: we need tourism, but the present price is too high.

## 4.1.2 Using statement prompts

The idea in this activity is to give students prompts in the form of statements (or simply words and phrases – see Example 2 below) as the basis for a text. In order to write the text, they have to perform several different kinds of operation (specified in Step 2 below) which will entail thinking about what the structure of their text will be and how they set about creating it.

You can vary the difficulty of the task and the type of text you want the students to create according to the kinds of prompts you provide.

This activity is also useful as a generating technique for starting students thinking about a topic if they are either not familiar with, or not confident about, brainstorming.

**Materials**

- *Either* find a short text suited to your students' interests and level and deconstruct it by writing each of its statements on separate slips of paper; *or* create a set of statements related to a topic which students have been studying (such as those in Example 1). Put the set of statements into an envelope, and have extra blank slips of paper available (you will need one set of statements for each group of students).

**Procedure**

1  Start students thinking about the topic covered by the set of statements with a brief warm-up discussion. Then give each group of students an envelope, pointing out that the statements they will find inside are not in any particular order.

2  Explain that they are to use the statements as the basis for a piece of writing, but that they are entirely free to decide how to order and use them. Suggest the following operations as a way of guiding the task:

Decide which statements are general ones and which supporting
Decide which statements can be grouped together
Decide what sort of text you could create from the ideas
Think about logical links between your groups of ideas
Decide on an order in which to deal with them
Add extra information or examples at appropriate points to clarify and
    elaborate upon the basic information (use extra slips of paper for this)

3  As the final stage, compare sequences and arrangements chosen by different groups. (If an OHP is available, it is relatively simple to display the results of each group's work by getting them to write out their sequence on an OHT. As you discuss each group's sequence, you can add suggestions for linking the ideas together.)

If some groups finish before others, suggest that they start drafting the opening paragraph of their text. Later, if you think sufficient interest has been generated, you could ask students to continue drafting a complete text.

Point out that the given statements are only *prompts* and that students should feel free to change the arrangement of ideas – and add new ones – as they write, if they find they want to.

Here are two examples illustrating tasks based on this technique.

*Example 1*

Here, students at a fairly advanced level worked on a discursive text with the title *The food scandal*. These were the statement prompts they were given:

The typical Western diet is the major cause of diseases leading to death in the West.
Diet is the main preventable cause of cancer and heart disease.
Changes in diet have reduced heart disease in the USA.
Britain has been slow to respond to dietary changes.
Good nutrition helps to prevent disease.
There is a conflict of interests between the food industry and a sensible food policy.
The public's ideas on nutrition are out-dated.
It is difficult for the public to obtain unbiased information on food.

This is how one group of students arranged and expanded upon these points (their own statements are in *italics*):

*Nutrition is one of the major problems which faces human life.*
The public's ideas on nutrition are out-dated.

It is difficult for the public to obtain unbiased information on food.
*The only source to get these information is from the advertisements which are not often convincing.*
There is a conflict of interests between the food industry and a sensible food policy.
*The health education is inadequate in many developing and some developed countries.*

The typical Western diet is the major cause of disease leading to death in the West.

Diet is the main preventable cause of cancer and heart disease.
*Food in the developing countries are more simple but insufficient. For example, instead of eating a complete meal, they eat much of one or two constituents because they are available in their country.*

Good nutrition helps to prevent disease.
*Because it contains all the constituents which the body needs in the right percentage.*
Changes in diet have reduced heart disease in the USA.
Britain has been slow to respond to dietary changes.

Later, they discussed how to make explicit the logical links between the ideas and clarified and exemplified some of the statements.

*Example 2*

In this second example, students at a much more elementary level used the technique for a narrative text. In this case, they were given simple word prompts – in random order – which indicated elements in the story:

| | | | |
|---|---|---|---|
| TV reporter | Work | Got up | Hospital |
| Bus | Breakfast | Nine o'clock news | Fire |

They first decided on a sequence for their story (i.e. what happened). Next they thought about the order in which they would deal with each prompt (not necessarily the same as the story sequence). The discussion involved in these two operations inevitably gave rise to suggestions about the circumstances of the events and the people concerned in them. The final stage, was to flesh out the skeleton of their story with details of characters, setting and events.

**4.1.3**
**Considering**
**priorities**

Many students are used to the idea of organising and planning points for a text, but in our experience, not so many think about why they decide to arrange their information as they do. Nor do they think about whether their 'plans' are appropriate to the particular writing task in hand.

In analytical or argumentative texts which discuss an issue or present a case, readers expect to be given a clear understanding of at least the following:
- The general background to the discussion or argument
- The specific issue or case being considered or argued
- The problems related to it, and possible solutions
- The writer's evaluation of these problems and solutions

However, it is not enough for writers merely to *include* all these elements; they must also decide what the priorities in a particular text are, and juggle the elements accordingly.

We suggest that you choose the structuring of a discursive text of the type mentioned above – the discussion of an issue, or the presentation of a case or point of view – as a task which will make students think about (a) the relative importance of their points and (b) how to make the structure of their text serve the development of the argument.

**Materials**

- Stimuli of various kinds on a controversial subject of interest to your students, and on which they will have differing opinions. Try to provide as great a range of stimuli as possible: written texts, visuals, recordings from TV and/or radio and so on. As a kind of mini-research project, you could ask the students to collect some of these materials themselves.
- Blank OHTs (if desired).

**Procedure**

1 We assume that the students will have started to generate ideas on the chosen topic in a previous session by discussing and making notes from the stimulus materials.

Begin this session by asking students to choose an aspect of the topic to write about – an *issue* which they would like to discuss, an *opinion* they would like to argue for or against, or a *case* they would like to present. For example, one class of students spent a session listening to a talk on the roots of violence in contemporary British society. They later watched a video and read a selection of articles which dealt with various aspects of the subject, a topic which proved very fruitful both in terms of the interest it aroused and the variety of issues the students chose to write about. Amongst these were the following:

A discussion of the psychological roots of male violence against women
An analysis of teenage violence in Japan

Arguments for and against the proposition 'Violent man is born, not made'
A discussion of the role which alcohol plays in violent behaviour

2 Explain to the students that the purpose of the text they are going to write is to discuss the issue they have chosen. Discuss with them what the reader expects of such a text, and put their suggestions on the board as a kind of 'macro-plan' for their own texts. Such a plan ought to include the following elements (though not, of course, necessarily in this order):
   (a) A clear presentation of the issue under discussion or the case to be argued (including background information if necessary)
   (b) Why the writer feels this issue to be worthy of concern
   (c) A review of arguments/opinions connected with the issue other than the writer's own
   (d) A clear understanding of the writer's own evaluation/opinion of the issue

3 Ask your students to think about which of these elements will take priority in their own texts, so that they can use this as a starting point for marshalling their ideas into a preliminary 'micro-plan'.
   Stress that the plan they create will depend very much upon what they want to say. It might, though, be helpful to review with them some possible schemes for organising information in these types of texts.

(a) **Discussing cause and effect:**
- cause —— effect

- $\text{cause}^1$
  $\text{cause}^2$ → effect
  $\text{cause}^3$

- cause → $\text{effect}^1$
  $\text{effect}^2$
  $\text{effect}^3$

- $\text{cause}^1$ — $\left\{\begin{matrix}\text{effect}^1\\\text{cause}^2\end{matrix}\right\}$ — $\left\{\begin{matrix}\text{effect}^2\\\text{cause}^3\end{matrix}\right\}$ —— $\text{effect}^3$

(b) **Discussing effect and cause:**
- effect —— cause

- $\text{effect}^1$
  $\text{effect}^2$ → cause
  $\text{effect}^3$

- effect → $\text{cause}^1$
  $\text{cause}^2$
  $\text{cause}^3$

- $\text{effect}^3$ — $\left\{\begin{matrix}\text{cause}^3\\\text{effect}^2\end{matrix}\right\}$ — $\left\{\begin{matrix}\text{cause}^2\\\text{effect}^1\end{matrix}\right\}$ —— $\text{cause}^1$

(c) **Listing aspects:**
- most important → least important
- least important → most important

(d) **Presenting arguments and counter-arguments:**
- presenting anticipated counter-arguments to one's own, refuting each in turn
- presenting one's own arguments in turn, together with anticipated counter-arguments
- listing all anticipated counter-arguments first, then all one's own arguments
- listing all one's own arguments first, then anticipated counter-arguments

(e) **Comparing and contrasting two (or more) situations:**

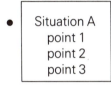

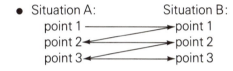

(f) **The SPRE/R scheme:**
Situation-Problem-Response-Evaluation/Result
(see 2.2.2: Variation 5 (p. 28))

4 To conclude this activity – and before they start drafting their texts – get the students to give progress reports. If they have been working individually, ask them to form groups of three or four; each person presents and explains their scheme to the others. If the students have been working in groups from the beginning, each group should present its scheme to the class (on OHP if possible).

During this 'talking-through' process, ask the other students/groups to make comments or suggestions or requests for clarification. Work out together how to incorporate these into the existing scheme.

*Example*

Here is an illustration of how one group of students decided to arrange their ideas in a text presenting an argument. They were one of the groups of Cypriot students who generated ideas on the topic *Smoking* (see 3.2.2 *Selecting and rejecting ideas*) (p. 55). Their text was to be in the form of an editorial arguing that more decisive action was needed in the campaign against smoking.

They started to sort out their ideas by thinking about the elements discussed in Step 2.

(a) Case to be argued?
  - There is far too much smoking in Cyprus — amongst men, women and especially young people
  - Something must be done to change this situation
(b) Why are we concerned?
  - People pay lip-service to the need for action to be taken, but no one takes it seriously
(c) Action taken to date?
  - There has been some attempt at government legislation on banning smoking in public places
(d) Our evaluation?
  - It has not been very successful, because fines are too low and people are not prosecuted because smoking does not yet have a negative image
  - Situation will not change until there is radical change of public opinion. Therefore, we need a much more effective anti-smoking campaign, especially among young people
  - We want to suggest action for such an anti-smoking campaign

They then decided that although most of what they wanted to say was in (d), in fact (b) was the most significant element. Their priority would therefore be to make this the theme of their editorial, inasmuch as it affected all other aspects of the situation. They decided to state this theme at the beginning.

They also tried to think about the logical relationships between the elements and decided upon the following scheme for starting a first draft.

(b) Why are we concerned?
  - People pay lip-service to the need for action to be taken, but no one takes it seriously
(a) As a result:
  - There is far too much smoking in Cyprus — amongst men, women and especially young people
  - Something must be done to change this situation
(c) Although
  - There has been some attempt at government legislation on banning smoking in public places
(d) yet
  1: It has not been very successful, because fines are too low and people are not prosecuted and because smoking does not yet have a negative image
(d) Therefore
  3: We want to suggest action for such an anti-smoking campaign
(d) Our conclusion:
  2: Situation will not change until there is radical change of public opinion. Therefore, we need a much more effective anti-smoking campaign, especially among young people

## 4.2 Experimenting with arrangements

This activity is designed to focus students' attention on the following:
(a) that there may not be a single 'best' way to organise information
(b) that the writer always has to be prepared to amend and change
   arrangements in order to include new ideas which arise in the course of
   composing.

**Materials**

- Handouts of short published texts to illustrate different ways of structuring
  and presenting the same basic information (see *Figure 26*).
- Ideas/notes/data for a text students will write, gathered or generated
  previously.
- Blank OHTs.

**Procedure**

1   You might like to lead into this activity by carrying out an analytical task
    with published texts to demonstrate how the same basic information can be
    organised differently to serve a variety of àudiences and purposes. Find two
    or three short articles on the same event or topic, but from different sources
    (see *Figure 26*), or use materials such as those suggested in
    3.2.1 *Variation 3: Eyewitness accounts* (p. 54).
        Get your students into small groups and assign each group one of the
    versions of the event. The group task is to analyse the way their text has
    dealt with the basic information. Put questions on the board to guide the
    discussion:

    Which idea is given greatest prominence?
    Do you think this idea provides a good focus for the text?
    Where is this key idea in the text?
    What information has the writer started the text with?
    How has the writer ended the text?

2   Compare the outcomes of these discussions and decide whether the
    different ways the texts have been structured is related to different
    audiences, purposes, attitudes and viewpoints.

3   Now turn to texts which the students themselves are going to write. We
    assume that they will be working with ideas or data that have been
    generated or gathered at some previous stage.
        Carry out the first part of the task as a whole class activity. Follow the
    kinds of preliminary grouping procedures suggested in 4.1.1 *Grouping ideas
    into framework* (p. 79), i.e.:
    - decide on dominant and supporting ideas
    - decide on categories/headings for grouping ideas
    so that the students end up with clusters of ideas or information, arranged
    in random order. Stress that any new ideas which arise as they are doing this
    should be included in appropriate places.

## THE INDEPENDENT

# Maggie lets in the rich

PREMIER Margaret Thatcher was last night preparing to offer a safe haven to the tycoons and mandarins of Hong Kong in the wake of the Peking massacre.

She hinted that wealthy businessmen and top civil servants may find their applications to settle in Britain treated favourably.

But she dismissed calls for all 3.25 million British nationals in the colony to be allowed to come here before the Chinese take over in 1997. That would more than double Britain's ethnic community.

Secret proposals suggest immigrants will have to show they have assets of over £150,000 before they are allowed in.

The hint came as Mrs Thatcher imposed an immediate ban on arms sales to China in protest at the bloodshed in Tiananmen Square.

Thousands of Chinese exiles throughout the world withdrew their life savings from the Bank of China.

But officials denied there was any panic and claimed there was no danger of the bank going under.

## British haven for people of Hong Kong ruled out

### By Colin Hughes
### Political Correspondent

The Government yesterday refused to offer a haven in Britain for the 3.25 million Hong Kong inhabitants who hold British nationality, should they want to leave when the colony reverts to China in 1997.

The Prime Minister told MPs that only 1.5 million new Commonwealth immigrants had been allowed into Britain since 1945. The Foreign Secretary added in a subsequent Commons statement that 3.25 million immigrants would, at a stroke, double the ethnic minority population in Britain.

But both Margaret Thatcher and Sir Geoffrey Howe agreed to interpret more flexibility in the existing immigration rules in the British Nationality Act 1981 in a move which could enable a few more thousand Hong Kong residents, notably public servants, to be granted right of abode in Britain. Sir Geoffrey also signalled a willingness to speed up direct elections to a representative assembly in Hong Kong, enabling democratic structures to be firmly in place before the Chinese take over.

At Commons Question Time Mrs Thatcher stepped up the Government's condemnation of the Chinese army's repression of peaceful rebellion, telling MPs of her "utter revulsion and outrage". She said the Government's "first and greatest concern has to be the people of Hong Kong". The Government's commitment to a secure future for those people was "as strong as ever", and she and Sir Geoffrey would look at ways in which they could be provided with reassurance.

However, the Prime Minister emphasised that 92 per cent of the territory would automatically revert to China when the British lease expired in 1997. There was nothing the Government could do to prevent that.

*Figure 26: Different ways of organising the same information – published texts*

Here, for example, are the idea-groups of some Cypriot students who were working on the topic 'Olives'.

---

physical description
- green/black varieties
- evergreen leaves
- gnarled trunks, ancient trees
- will grow in hot, arid conditions
- method of cultivation

uses in cooking
- oil
- flavouring
- essential ingredient for traditional dishes
- salads, mayonnaise
- bread/cakes
- frying fish

contribution to diet
- healthy snack
- nutritious
- high in mono-unsaturated fats

OLIVES

value to economy
- export of olives
- export of olive oil
- carving for tourists
- don't require much irrigation

contribution to culture
- part of landscape (terraces)
- shade for flocks
- firewood
- wood used for artefacts
- customs + festivals associated with harvesting and planting
- regional variations of flavour of oil
- link with past: traditional cultivation

symbolic significance
- peace
- fertility
- harmony
- beauty

---

4   Since the point of this activity is to focus on different ways of arranging the same information, divide the class into small groups now, and ask each group to decide how they are going to arrange the clusters of ideas they produced in Step 2. In order to do this, they will have to imagine a context for their text (i.e. a purpose, audience and form). They will also have to think about the following:
(a) the reasons for choosing one order rather than another
(b) the logical connections between the idea-groups.
They should note down what these connections are and try to think of

suitable connective expressions which could eventually function as discourse markers in their texts.

Encourage the groups to try out different options on arranging the information, and to decide which they find most appropriate and satisfactory.

If they sketch out their various arrangements on OHTs, it will make their subsequent presentation to the rest of the class easier. If OHP equipment is not available, making copies of each group's arrangements, or getting them written up on the board will work equally well. The idea is to compare the arrangements and discuss both the merits and drawbacks of each.

*Example*

As an illustration of how this task worked in practice, let us look at notes made by one of the groups working on *Olives*.

They first of all decided that their purpose was to explain the importance of olives in Cypriot culture to a non-Cypriot reader, and then discussed two possible arrangements of the ideas they started with in Step 2:

**Alternative 1**

| Train of thought | Idea cluster | |
|---|---|---|
| What are olives? | → Physical description | |
| Why are they important to us? Many reasons. although most foreigners associate them only with cooking and food | → Uses in cooking | |
| And indeed, they are very healthy. | → Contribution to diet | details as in Step 2 |
| Besides that, though, they are valuable in our economy. | → Value to economy | |
| Many foreigners, however, are not aware of their part in our culture and traditions | → Contribution to culture | |
| Neither are they aware that they are symbols for us | → Symbolic significance | |

**Alternative 2**

| Train of thought | Idea cluster |
|---|---|

We are Mediterranean people: olives are vital to our culture

→ Contribution to culture
Physical description

They are equally important for cooking
Moreover, they are very healthy

→ Uses in cooking

→ Contribution to diet

However, we are also Cypriot people: olives are vital to our economy

→ Value to economy

In these ways, olives have always been so important to our culture that they have become symbols

→ Symbolic significance

} details as in Step 2

The group decided they liked Alternative 2 better than Alternative 1, because it made clearer to a non-Cypriot reader the significance of olives in the Cypriot culture. They subsequently used this arrangement of ideas as a starting point for a first draft.

## 4.3 Relating structure to focal idea

The emphasis in this activity is on showing how a theme or focal idea that has been identified (see 3.1 *Discovering main ideas* and 3.2 *Considering purpose*) gives a good lead for thinking about how to structure the text. We suggest that you work here on the sort of texts in which the reader expects to find certain elements, but not necessarily in any fixed order. Two such types are:

(a)  recounting a personal anecdote

(b)  writing about people's lives and achievements.

The structure of the text will depend upon what the writer perceives to be its most significant element, and upon how they decide to focus the reader's attention on this element.

**4.3.1 Personal anecdotes**

**Materials**

● A taped oral anecdote, and copies of the transcript, if possible.

**Procedure**

1  Stress to the students that they have to assume their reader to be someone who does not know anything (or who has, at best, minimal knowledge) about the experience they are going to recount. They will therefore have to imagine the questions the reader would like to have answered.

Spend a few minutes discussing the sorts of experiences people often feel they want to share with readers. Ask them to think of experiences they have had which they consider a reader would find interesting (see also 3.2.4 *Transforming personal experiences* (p. 58).

2  Compile on the board/OHP a list of suggestions for the sorts of information the reader will want to know. This would probably include the following elements:
   ● Background/context of the experience
   ● Characters involved
   ● Events which took place
   ● Effects events had on characters/situation
   ● What was remarkable/interesting/noteworthy about the experience
   ● The writer's reactions to, or feelings about, the experience

3  The next step is for the students to decide which of these elements is the most interesting or significant in the particular case they are going to write about; in other words, how they are going to focus their text and structure all the other information around this key idea.

To help them do this, you could provide some kind of stimulus text to set them thinking. We have found it useful and motivating to use oral accounts of experiences as a stimulus. Find a suitable recorded anecdote (conversation with friends, off-air radio recording or published materials) and play it to your students. Ask them to think about:
   ● why the narrator told the story
   ● what point the narrator was trying to make
   ● whether, if they were asked to write an account of the story, they would use this point as the focus.

If you can provide a transcript (as in the Example on the next page, so much the better. The students will then be able to make notes under the headings of the elements discussed in Step 2 above and decide how they would use this information in a written account:

- Would they use the same sequence as the oral narrator?
- How could they convey in written language the points that the speaker made with intonation, stress, pausing, change of pitch and so on?
- Which of the elements would they begin with?
- How would they end?

An alternative is to ask one or two students to tell the class orally about the personal experience they have chosen to write about (or you can get the students to work in pairs). The listeners make suggestions about which aspect of the experience struck them most forcefully as they listened, and which could therefore be the focus of the written text.

4  When they turn to their own texts, suggest that the students:
  (a) make notes and collect ideas under the 'element' headings suggested in Step 2 above
  (b) decide which of the elements is to be used as the focus
  (c) decide how to incorporate the other elements.
     Encourage the students to think about various options before deciding which arrangement is most effective. You could provide a few questions to guide them such as:

Will you use a chronological sequence?
Will you start from the final point of the experience and work backwards?
Will you start with the events and reveal the background later?
Will you start with the background and lead into the events?
Will you withhold certain information until the end to provide a surprise?

*Example*

On the next page you will see the transcript of a sample oral narrative which could be used as a stimulus for writing about personal experiences, as suggested in Step 3 above. If you used such a narrative, you would probably want your students to discuss:

- the various elements of the story, and how the *speaker* has chosen to present them to the listeners
- whether this same presentation would work in a *written* account of the incident
- the thesis or point of the story
- what changes of grammar, vocabulary, style and organisation would have to be made if the story were to be incorporated into a written text
- what point or thesis the story could be used to illustrate.

### The bank story

The story comes from an unedited radio conversation programme. Just before the speaker tells the story, the conversation has been on the subject of inventing stories and games by computer.

(Symbols used in the transcript:

| | | |
|---|---|---|
| +, ++, +++ | = | pauses of varying length |
| upper case [e.g. *WORKing*] | = | stressed syllable |
| ↓ or ↑ | = | movement of pitch upward or downward) |

---

I've just started WORKing on one which is + um + um + where the ↑ major obJECTive of the gaa it's called buREAUcracy the major obJECTive of the game is actually + to get your BANK to acknowledge a change of adDRESS card + um + (laughter) ↑ this will lead you from one + ↑ one + HUGE EPic adventure to anOTHer though in fa though the the the ONE thing that's imPELLing you is just TRYing to get your bank to DO this + ↑ this actually CAME from something that occurred to me when I when I MOVED to my current FLAT I got a mortgage from the BANK + er + but nevertheless when I was sending OUT a change of address card I thought well I'd better send them one ANYway they SHOULD know I'm here because they're PAYing for it + um ++ ↑ um + and the next statement I got was + sent to my old adDRESS so I sent them an ↑ OTHer change of address card and the next statement after THAT was sent to my old adDRESS ↑ so I WROTE them a letter saying look you ↑ MUST know I'm here because you're ↑ INto this flat for x numbers of thousands of pounds ++ um + I've SENT you two changes of address cards + um + ↑ PLEASE will you sort of UPdate your records and make sure you send stuff to my new adDRESS + ↑ so they wrote me back a very + um + a ↑ POLoGETic letter saying we DO realise this is VERy silly I'm VEry sorry it won't happen again +++ ↓ GUESS where they sent the LETter ++ (laughter)

---

## 4.3.2
## People's lives and achievements

**Materials**

- Files of information about famous people – either historical or contemporary figures. The wider you can make the range of sources for the materials (including TV and radio recordings) the more stimulating the activity. You could get your students to collect some of these materials as part of a project integrated with other aspects of their course. (Keep the materials which prove to be successful and build up a library of such files to have on hand for use with future classes.)

**Procedure**

1 Spend a few minutes considering the sorts of things we like to find out about people when we read accounts of their lives and achievements. Compile a list of suggestions on the board/OHP, which would probably include:

important/significant/interesting events in person's life
context of person's life (historical, geographical, socio-economic
    background)
career and education
achievements and failings
beliefs
aims/goals
personality/character
relations with other people.

2 If you wish, you could look at one or two sample texts to set students thinking about how they could arrange these elements in a written account – an interesting obituary, or a short article such as the sample texts in *Figures 27* and *28*. Analyse them with your students to find out:
- which of the elements listed above in Step 1 the writer has included
- which element provides the text with a theme or focus
- how the other elements are organised around this focal idea.

3 When they turn to their own texts, they make notes from the information file on the person they are going to write about under the 'element' headings suggested in Step 1 above, and then consider which element will provide the most interesting focus for their text. The following questions might help them decide about an effective structure:

How much of your text will you devote to the element you have decided is
    most important?
Will you deal with the concrete aspects of the person's life (i.e. its
    historical, geographical, socio-economic context) before the more
    abstract elements (i.e. goals, achievements/beliefs/personality) or *vice
    versa*?
Will you start with your most important element, or leave it till last?

# Raymond Tongue

Ray Tongue's untimely death has been the cause of personal sadness as well as being a very real loss to IATEFL and to the profession as a whole. While the officers of an association can be replaced, no one can replace a person who was regarded with so much affection and respect.

Born in Birmingham, Ray Tongue saw service in the War before taking an honours degree at Oxford, after which he worked as Deputy Principal of the Joint Services School for Linguists. A period as Academic Registrar at the then University College of Ibadan, Nigeria was his first overseas posting before joining the British Council in 1958, and from then on virtually all of his career was outside Europe.

Beginning in Thailand, he moved to posts in Zaire, Singapore, Hyderabad, and Hong Kong before ending his Council career as Education Adviser at the Commission of the European Communities in Brussels.

During his time in Singapore, he published an important study on one of the so-called New Englishes, with his book, *The English of Singapore and Malaysia*, followed several years later by a related title, *Indian and British English*. For his contributions to the advancement of ELT in South East Asia, he was awarded the OBE in 1974.

Following his retirement from the British Council in 1984, he remained extremely active in ELT, joining the panel of inspectors for the Recognition Scheme as well as becoming Treasurer of IATEFL and, assisted by his wife, Agnes, taking on the role of Conference Organiser for the Edinburgh and Warwick conferences. It is probably in this latter capacity that Ray's particular combination of organisational and people skills became most widely known.

Ray had the wonderful ability to make everyone he worked with feel valued and respected. As Chairman of IATEFL, I found his wisdom, born of years of experience, to be of enormous value, while his never failing sense of humour cut many problems down to size. Ray could always be relied upon to give good council and encouragement and it is difficult to imagine him no longer being at the end of the phone to give such advice, or not being present as a contributor to sane discussion in committee. We all miss him.

*Raymond Kenneth Tongue, born 3 December 1924, died 25 April, 1989.*

*Figure 27: 'Obituary' sample text*

Bourke-White was the daughter of an engineer and inventor who grew into a world where images of industry seemed as symbolic of human progress in the USA as they were in Soviet Russia. The Five Year Plans and the spirit that became the New Deal both fostered the romantic belief in salvation through steel.

By 1928 Bourke-White was a top industrial photographer and, although her images convey perhaps a rather too simple faith in the beauty of their subject matter, they are impressively well composed.

Before she produced her famous first cover for *Life* - a photograph of Fort Peck Dam - she had begun to extend her range. She collaborated with Erskine Caldwell (whom she later married) on a book about Southern poverty.

Bourke-White was appropriately an idealist who thought that photography could change the world. The Munich crisis found her in Czechoslovakia, and the pictures she gained there made her naively certain that a free Press, with its photographs, might have stifled fascism. If there was to be a war she was determined to be there, "to make folks see just how horrible war is - and perhaps I shall have done my little bit towards ending wars for all time". She would be as good as her word, however ingenuous her hopes.

She became a public heroine, and even a national pin-up when photographed in a flying suit, but she aroused resentment in some male colleagues who thought her success was mostly due to her use of feminine charm.

Her most notable war pictures were of ruined Europe in the wake of the German retreat - the death camps and other harrowing scenes. After a spell in India there was soon another war, in Korea, where she took an unblinking shot of a severed head being appraised with cheerful satisfaction by the executioner.

Bourke-White then reverted to her early abstraction, but now in aerial views of landscape, many in colour. And though Parkinson's Disease soon put an end to her career, she allowed a photo feature to be made of her fight for recovery after brain surgeons had attempted unsuccessfully to cure her.

Margaret Bourke-White certainly deserves our admiration. Perhaps she hadn't quite the (rather malign) genius of Germany's Leni Riefenstahl, but she was a great photojournalist, if not a photographer of the very first rank. And more than 50 years ago, she showed how much a spirited woman could achieve in a man's world if she believed that new deals of all kinds were possible.

## Camera Woman

**Margaret Bourke-White** was a unique heroine of the camera. She was the first woman industrial photographer of any note. Responsible for the first cover of *Life* magazine in 1936, she was an intrepid photojournalist who, in her time, covered the poverty of the Deep South, the drama of the first Five Year Plan in Russia - as well as the Second World War and its aftermath. On top of all this, she pioneered the notion of aerial photographs to be enjoyed as near-abstractions.

*Figure 28: 'Lives and achievements' sample text*

# 5

# Drafting

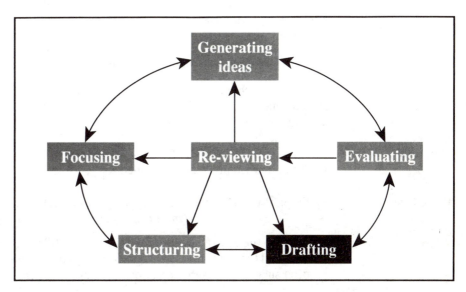

*He being immersed in phrases painfully consenting, it was like darting fish with hooks in their gills, dragged from the depths of an unplumbed pool . . .*

Many of the activities described in earlier sections are often classified as 'pre-writing', although as will have been clear, all of them are in fact part of the *writing* process. Activities in this section mark the move from the so-called pre-writing stage to actually writing a first draft, even if, as in fastwriting and loopwriting, stretches of text have already been produced. The tasks you set your students will vary according to what you wish to focus on, and they could probably range from parts of texts, or shorter pieces of writing such as the mini-saga – as in some of the examples given below – to longer, complete essays or papers.

Because writers are now making the transition from the *writer-based* writing of the earlier idea-generating and theme-identifying phases to the *reader-based* writing which will constitute the final product, the concerns of the reader should now begin to assume more significance. In addition to considering how best to organise information and ideas for their reader, writers now have to think of how to attract the attention of their audience, how to continue appealing to them, and how to lead them through the text to a conclusion which, often by referring directly or indirectly to the opening, ends the text with a sense of completion.

Fundamental to the approach to writing which we are presenting here are the processes of revision and rewriting. We would advocate running through the 'write-revise-rewrite' cycle at least once for most writing tasks, and, when both teacher and students desire to have a product that is as good as they can make it, twice through the cycle is recommended. This will mean that the students will write three drafts, of which the third is the final product. However, as can be attested by anyone who has had to write anything really important for publication, many more than three drafts may be required, even if successive drafts are more and more similar. Fortunately, the drudgery of such redrafting is greatly relieved by the word processor. Indeed, the word processor and a process approach to writing might almost have been made for each other.

## 5.1 Drafting by the teacher ▶

As with all teacher demonstrations, this activity is to help reveal the process to the students, who will also appreciate that even for teachers, writing can be difficult.

**Materials**
- Notes on OHT or poster from earlier generating stages.
- Optional word processor and video rig.

**Procedure**

1  Display notes from earlier stages, i.e. from 2.1.1 *Brainstorming by the teacher* and 3.1.2, *Variation 1: Loopwriting by the teacher*.

2  Refer to the central idea which you have identified as the thesis for your text, and then try out several different ways of beginning, asking students to offer suggestions. Write these on the board or OHT.

3  Choose the opening that seems most appealing or interesting and continue writing. Talk about the choices that you are having to make at each stage and how a decision made at one point has implications for the way your text develops at others.

4  To make the process more interactive, you can involve the students by getting them to suggest how to continue the draft. Indeed, it is important to show that you face decisions, just as they do, about how to organise ideas, how to develop them and how to continue the text.

*Example 1*

This example, which was composed using a word processor linked to a large VDU monitor visible to the class (see *Introduction* pp. 9–10), is based on the ideas and thesis dealt with in the examples in 2.1.1 *Brainstorming by the teacher* (p. 19) and 3.1.2, *Variation 1: Loopwriting by the teacher* (p. 47). This is not a final draft; work will still need to be done on improving the rather self-conscious expression and vocabulary, e.g. *the architectural legacy of elitism*.

**Life in Cities**

The train halted. Anxiously, I peered out of the door. Lots of people, but no sign of anyone who might be looking for me. So I climbed down and, with my suitcase, walked towards the exit. Stepping out under the porch, I caught my breath. In front of me was a busy, sparkling stretch of water, lapping a coastline dominated by half-familiar buildings of architectural eminence. I had arrived in Istanbul, the sometime capital of Byzantium and now, in this one stunning moment which I could never repeat, there it was, spread out before me under a clear blue sky.

The drama of the skyline of Istanbul, the very tangible sense of layer upon layer of history, stretching from classical to modern times, summarizes the key feature of the city and city life. Cities have always been the seat of power and influence from the time when mankind first established urban civilization. Rulers, whether priests or kings, were the focus around which a court assembled, and patronage of the arts ensured that the city became the artistic expression of that civilization.

Whatever criticisms can be levelled at such concentrations of power, the architectural legacy of elitism is the very thing that makes cities such interesting and exciting places to live in. Who could deny the splendour and elegance of Paris? And who could have produced such elegance but an essentially autocratic monarchy and the ruling class assembled around it?

In our more egalitarian times, the city fathers have to attend to the daily needs of the masses, and running a modern city is a demanding operation of enormous complexity which most of us take for granted – until something goes wrong. We assume that the garbage will be collected and pavements swept, that buses and the metro will run on schedule, that phones will ring, water will flow, traffic will circulate, that shops will be stocked and that our urban routines will continue on their accustomed course. For these are all of the amenities which city life should offer, and it is only when the garbage collectors go on strike or the transport system falters that we recognize the intricacy of the urban civilization in which we live.

Meanwhile, at the station in Istanbul, my friends arrived, and later dropped me off at the Galata bridge, where, as I crossed, I felt a slight thrill at being in the centre of such a significant city poised at the meeting point of Asia and Europe. Maybe some of the city's former glory, on closer acquaintance, proved to be a little tarnished. And perhaps one might have wished for less noise and pollution. But here was represented the variety, spectacle, noise, bustle, danger and excitement epitomizing life in cities – that most significant expression of human civilization.

Among the decisions which the writer had to make were:

1 How to open the essay in an interesting way which would gain a reader's attention and interest. (Paragraph 1).
2 How to move from the narrative opening in Istanbul, which deals with a particular place and event, to the more general idea of cities and their history (Paragraph 2).
3 How to show that the works of the powerful have benefits for everybody (Paragraph 3).
4 How to develop further the idea of the ordinary person and the way city life affects them (Paragraph 4).

5 How to return to the stranded traveller in Istanbul so as not to leave the reader wondering what had happened to him; yet at the same time, clearly establish the main point of the essay (Paragraph 5).

*Example 2*

A teacher in Luxembourg, Elizabeth Goletti, planned a series of lessons in which she and a colleague each wrote a first draft, evaluated it, and rewrote it, together with their students, to provide a role model. Here are some of her comments on the exercise:

> '. . . Believe me, the students were gleeful at the opportunity to pick apart the adults' essays . . .'
> '. . . The entire process took about four hours, i.e. four class periods and two homework assignments. All this for approximately a hundred words per student! . . .'
> '. . . This was the first time the students saw adults chewing their pencils and struggling to write. I believe the students learned a great deal from the experiment. I certainly learned the fear of making a fool of myself!'

## 5.2  Beginning, adding, ending

It is said that the two most critical and exacting manoeuvres in flying are taking off and landing, and the same is true of writing. A good beginning will attract the reader's attention; a good ending will send the reader away satisfied and stimulated.

Less exciting, though no less important, than taking off and landing is the business of staying airborne. As a pilot has to keep the craft and its passengers safely in the air, so a writer has to keep the text flowing and sustain the reader's interest. Part of this task will involve filling out a text already written – a skill that is probably rarely practised, but one that is essential to successful writing.

**5.2.1** ○
**Beginning and ending effectively**

The basic procedure here (Steps 1 to 3) is intended to be repeated with different types of writing, but only one type should be dealt with at a time. We suggest that you have to hand examples of various types of text, and every so often slot the activity into an odd ten minutes or so at the end of some other task, dealing with a different type of writing each time. Or you may decide to cover a number of text-types in one lesson, though it would not be advisable to attempt to deal with them all.

**Materials**

- Text-type files, as in 3.4.1 *Comparing characteristics of text-types* (p. 75)
- Handouts of sample texts of various types
- Students' own drafts (for Step 4)

**Procedure**

1 On the board or OHT, write students' suggestions as to what they expect from the beginning and ending of the sort of text they are going to consider.

2 Get students into small groups (twos or threes) and distribute sample texts. Preferably there should be more than one sample text per type, and if there are several samples, let each group work on a different text.

Ask students to consider the characteristics of the beginning and ending of their text and the kinds of ideas they contain. They should also decide whether they are satisfactory or not. Here are some questions to guide discussion:

Is the opening interesting?
What form does it take? e.g. is it a quotation, a statement or
   generalisation, an anecdote?
How is the opening related to the rest of the text?
How is the ending linked to the opening?
How is the ending linked to the rest of the text?

3   Invite each group in turn to contribute their ideas from the discussion in Step 2, and to compare them with the list on the board/OHP in Step 1. Students can then note the typical characteristics of beginnings and endings of this particular type on a chart, and add the sample text they have discussed to their text-type file (see 3.4.1 *Comparing characteristics of text-types*). If any of the texts were felt to have particularly unsatisfactory beginnings or endings, students could discuss the reasons for this.

4   If students themselves have been working on a draft or a text which falls into the category discussed in the previous stages of this activity, they can evaluate the beginning and ending of their own drafts in terms of the criteria they have established in Step 3 above, changing and amending them where necessary.

**5.2.2
Considering
ways of
beginning**

Finding a good way to start a text is not easy, for it must fulfil two conditions: it must be appropriate for the type of writing concerned, and it must make the reader want to read on. In this activity, students look at various ploys for whetting the appetite of the audience.

**Materials**

● Handouts or a poster/OHT with opening sentences and paragraphs from a variety of published texts.

**Procedure**

1   Before referring to the openings you have chosen, ask students to suggest what it is that grabs their attention when they are scanning a newspaper or magazine, or a book in the library or bookshop. Ask them also to recall the openings of stories or articles they have read: what was it in the opening that caught their attention?

2   Refer to the examples you have provided, and note any similarities with the examples given by students. Then ask them, either individually, or in pairs or groups, to:
(a)  choose an opening that interests them
(b)  say what it is that has caught their attention
(c)  suggest how the text will probably continue.

3   Turn the students' attention to their own writing. Ask them to write an opening to any piece they have begun in earlier idea-generating activities.

4   Now have students compare with each other the openings which they have written. They should ask themselves, *Do I want to continue reading?* If the

*Example*

Here is a selection of openings.

(a) In a broad Moscow street not two hundred yards from the Leningrad station, on the upper floor of an ornate and hideous hotel built by Stalin in the style known to Muscovites as Empire During the Plague, the British Council's first ever audio fair for the teaching of the English language and the spread of British culture was grinding to its excruciating end.

(John le Carré The Russia House Hodder & Stoughton 1989)

(b) If it takes more than 200 gallons of paint to paint a jumbo jet, how many family motor cars would that same paint cover? The answer is – 110.

(Painting the Jumbo High Life British Airways, April 1989)

(c) Modern Times began in 1776.

(L K Setright Revolutions Car Magazine, November 1989)

(d) The radio report the evening before had been terse and ominous: gale warnings for the northern Labrador Sea. Our apprehension was over more than heavy seas, however. There were icebergs ahead – and we would be steaming into those waters in darkness, straight into a picket line of ice the size of cathedrals, borne slowly south on the Canadian Current.

(Barry Lopez Arctic Dreams Macmillan 1986, paperback edition Pan Books 1987)

(e) 'It is therefore ordered and adjudged by this Court, that you be transported upon the seas, beyond the seas, to such a place as His Majesty, by the advice of His Privy Council, shall think fit to direct and appoint, for the term of your natural life.' Or seven years, or fourteen – in any case, the shock of sentencing was dreadful. In law, seven years' banishment meant what it said; but what man could be certain of returning to England at the end of it? For many people, the sentence of transportation – whatever its announced length – must have seemed like a one-way trip over the edge of the world.

(Robert Hughes The Fatal Shore Collins Harvill 1987, Pan Books 1988)

These are some of the points to be noted about the openings in a class discussion.

Example (a) is the beginning of a narrative, with considerable circumstantial detail, leading readers to wonder who is involved in the event that is reaching its 'excrutiating end'. The only way to satisfy their curiosity is to read on.

Example (b) attracts the reader with an unusual rhetorical question. Having found the answer in the next sentence, readers may now wish to read on to find if there are any other interesting pieces of information about the subject of the article: painting jumbo jets, such as the one they may well be travelling in as they read their in-flight magazine.

Example (c) begins with a flat assertion which almost challenges the reader, who may now want to read further to find some evidence or argument to back up the writer's bold claim.

answer is *no*, they should discuss this with the writer and jointly try to find a way of beginning which will motivate the reader to continue reading.

Example (d) is another narrative which begins with a sense of imminent danger so that the reader may feel drawn on to find out what happened to the author and his fellow voyagers as they sailed into the night.

Example (e) uses an arresting quotation which, with its archaic and legal style, dramatises the plight of people sentenced to transportation to the penal colony of New South Wales, thus drawing the reader into the writer's subject: the voyage out.

Variation 1:
Matching openings
and methods

**Materials**

- A handout in which examples of beginnings and a list of the methods of beginning are presented in mismatched order (see the example below – though note that here the openings and methods are *not* in mismatched order: you would have to mix them up for the handout).
- Students' own drafts.

**Procedure**

1 Follow essentially the same procedure as in 5.2.2 *Considering ways of beginning*, with the addition that you ask students to match the examples to the method.
2 Having studied these examples, have students apply one of the methods to their own drafts by writing an opening which most effectively begins their text.

*Example*

Here are various ways of beginning an essay on *Life in Cities*.

| Method | Example |
|---|---|
| Fact | Sao Paolo in Brazil is the fastest growing city in Latin America. |
| Opinion | Cities such as Rio provide the most striking juxtaposition of wealth and poverty. |
| Event | The pilot's voice came over the intercom, drawing our attention to the City of London below and as we craned our necks to look out of the window, we could see the Tower of London, St Paul's Cathedral and the Palace of Westminster below us, like models in a toy town. |
| Speech | 'This is the captain speaking,' said a voice over the intercom. 'Below us you will see the City of London.' |
| Anecdote | It had been a terrible journey, with delays at every stage and we finally arrived at our hotel some time after midnight. Naturally, the kitchen staff had gone home, but we scouted around and eventually found a Lebanese restaurant that was still open, thus confirming my faith that you can find somewhere to eat in any city, no matter what the time of day. |
| Quotation | It was Shelley who said that 'Hell is a city much like London.' |

Variation 2:
Bad openings

Give your students some examples of *bad* opening sentences of novels and discuss why they are bad – banality of topic, irrelevant information, overload of assumed knowledge, and so on. In some cases, there will be linguistic clues to such features. For instance, in Example 3 below, the frequency of the past perfect tense is related to the assumed knowledge which the writer draws upon – but which, of course, the reader has no way of sharing at this point in the story. The follow-up to such discussion could be a competition to write more bad openings.

*Examples: Bad
opening sentences**

(a) 'The variety of quirks, ailments and miscellaneous disfigurements that can strike the average supermarket cart is truly amazing,' she said.

(b) It was autumn, and the fog clung to the old house as it did every autumn (with the exception of the previous year, which had been incredibly sunny) like damp gauze on a soldier's wound, except there was no blood, as he stopped the car at the kerb and gazed thoughtfully towards the house.

(c) It came to him in a cocaine rush as he took the Langley exit that if Aldrick had told Filipov about Hancock only Tulfgengian could have known that the photograph which Wagner had shown to Maximov on the jolting *S-bahn* was not the photograph of Kessler that Bradford had found at the dark, sinister house in the Schillerstrasse the day that Straub told Percival that the man on the bridge had not been Aksakov but Pavstovsky, which meant that it was not Kleist but Kurger that Cerenesky had met in the bleak, wintry Grünewald and that, therefore, only Frau Epp could have known that Muller had followed Droyson to the steamy aromatic cafe in the Beethovenstrasse where he had told Bürger that Todrov had known since the Liebermann affair that McIntyre had not met Stoltz at the Golitzer Bahnhof but instead had met Sommer in the cavernous Ahnlater Bahnhof.

**5.2.3
Considering
ways of ending**

The activities here obviously tie in closely with those in 5.2.2 *Considering ways of beginning* above, but whereas in 5.2.2 the focus is on finding an arresting opening for a text, here it is on bringing it to a satisfying close. Successful pieces of writing have a sense of wholeness about them, and in our experience, many students find it difficult to link the conclusion of their text both with its opening and its thesis in a way that is interesting and decisive.

**Materials**

● A worksheet containing mismatched examples of openings and endings (see the example opposite).

**Procedure**

1  Issue the worksheet to students, with instructions to match openings and endings.

2  Compare the matchings the students have made, and analyse the ways in which the endings reflect or relate to the openings.

* The examples are taken from Stephen Pile (1988) *The return of heroic failures*. He, in turn, is quoting from a competition run by Professor Scott Rice of the San Jose State University, whose annual Bulwer-Lytton contest these examples come from.

*Example*

## Beginnings

(a) Edinburgh is a city unlike any other. It has been called 'The Athens of the North' and had its site compared with the seven hills on which Rome was built. But Athens ('the Edinburgh of the South') is in truth not more dramatic to look at and if you search diligently you can find at least a dozen hills within the Edinburgh boundaries and a hundred or so within an hour's drive.

(*Edinburgh, Official Guide* City of Edinburgh District Council)

(b) Have you ever stood at the supermarket checkout and inwardly tut-tutted at the white sliced bread, sausages, sugary jam and tinned spaghetti filling up the basket next to yours? If so, the likelihood is that you have never had to feed a family on income support.

(Kate de Selincourt, Supermarket shelves that are out of reach, *The Independent* 24 October 1989)

(c) The train came out of the red horizon and bore down towards them over the single straight track.

(Nadine Gordimer *No Place Like: Selected short stories* Penguin 1978, The train from Rhodesia)

(d) Most journeys begin less abruptly than they end, and to fix the true beginning of this one in either time or space is a task which I do not care to undertake. I find it easier to open my account of it at the moment when I first realised, with a small shock of pleasure and surprise, that it had actually begun.

(Peter Flemming *News from Tartary* Jonathan Cape and Futura 1980)

(e) Getting on for 40 billion colour photographs are printed every year, a third of them in America, and most of them show happy families and smiling faces on holiday.

(David Taylor, Have you got a film in? *High Life*, British Airways 1989)

## Endings

(i) The train had cast the station like a skin. It called out to the sky, I'm coming, I'm coming; and again, there was no answer.

(ii) 'That's that,' said Kini, and sighed. The journey was over.

(iii) The authority is now developing ideas for an information pack on healthy eating on a low budget. But authority workers may be facing the task with heavy hearts, knowing that for people such as the four million British adults and children who depend on income support, and others on low incomes, a healthy diet will be priced beyond their reach.

(iv) You pays your money and your takes your innovatory choice. If we go on taking stills at the rate of 40 billion a year and making enough videotape to spool from here to Mars, there ought to be room for everyone.

(v) The star of all events, however, is undoubtedly the city itself. A magnificent setting, fine buildings, a wealth of green space, with ever-changing views to the hills, the river and the sea make it a town of constant discovery and delight, historically and contemporaneously fascinating. Edinburgh is, in the truest sense of the word, unique.

| | |
|---|---|
| Variation: Completing texts | You could use this procedure with a variety of text-types, depending on the type of writing you are dealing with in a particular class. The principle is a simple one: you supply students with an incomplete text and they have to complete it, bearing in mind the sorts of considerations that were discussed in 5.2.1 *Beginning and ending effectively* above. |

If, for instance, you were considering narrative types, you could have students enact a role play based on a short story, as described in 2.5 *Using role play/simulation* (p. 42). Then give them an incomplete version of the story, which develops the ideas embodied in the role play. Invite them to complete the story in line with the development of characters, plot and theme exemplified in the excerpt you have given them. Subsequently, they compare the way they have completed the story, both with each other and with the original version.

## 5.2.4 Adding information

**Materials**

- Student drafts or texts you have prepared, to be used as the basis for handouts.
- Tasksheets or OHTs (see Step 2 below).

**Procedure**

1 Collect examples of students' drafts and analyse them in advance of the lesson to identify points at which new or extra information is needed. Keep in mind the assumed readers and their knowledge of the subject. If certain knowledge cannot be assumed and is not present in the text, then it will almost certainly need to be added.

2 Prepare two worksheets or OHTs: on Worksheet A, put the original text; on Worksheet B, write the additional information, though not in the same sequence as it will be included in the text.

3 Present or display texts (Worksheet A) and ask students, working either as a whole class or in groups, to:
   - consider what the reader already knows about the subject
   - think of what information the reader needs to know to make sense of the text
   - identify missing information
   - suggest where such information could be added.

4 Hand out or display the additional information (Worksheet B) and ask students to:
   - add the new information at appropriate points in the text
   - say what changes they will have to make in order to accommodate it
   - rewrite the text, incorporating the new information.

*Example*

This example illustrates how the above procedures worked with some Indonesian students who, in groups of four, had prepared descriptions of local production processes.

Here is the original text of one of the groups:

> How rice is produced
> The rice seeds are sown on the rice bed. The ground is prepared. The seedlings are transplanted into the rice fields. The rice is weeded. After fifty days the rice is harvested, then it is dried. And then it is milled. After that it is cooked and it is served with fish, meats and vegetables.

And here is the additional information, prepared by the teacher:

> Rice is used as the basis of many Indonesian dishes.
> In some regions, two or three rice crops a year are grown.
> The fields must be irrigated.
> The growing season lasts from four to six months.

Below is the second version of the text with the information incorporated. The teacher pointed out to the group concerned that further changes would be needed to make the text more cohesive. Also, the information could have been added at points other than those they had chosen.

> In some regions two or three rice crops a year are grown. The growing season lasts from four to six months. The ground is prepared. The rice seeds are sown on the rice bed. The seedlings are transplanted into the rice fields. The fields must be irrigated. The rice is weeded. After fifty days the rice is harvested, then it is dried. And then it is milled. After that it is cooked and it is served with fish, meats and vegetables. Rice is used as the basis of many Indonesian dishes.

**Variation 1: Students supply information**

The basic procedure is as in 5.2.4, but in this case, do not prepare Worksheet B. Instead, have students themselves prepare the additional information. Thus, Step 3 will be as follows:

3   Present or display texts and ask students, working either as a whole class or in groups, to discuss answers to the questions below and to rewrite the text so as to incorporate the improvements suggested by their discussion:

What does the reader already know about the subject?
What information will the reader need to know to make sense of the text?
What specific information is missing?
Where should such information be added?

**Variation 2:
Enlisting the help
of the word
processor**

If the students have prepared the first draft on a word processor, they can incorporate the additional information at agreed points in the text, save the new version and print it out. As the word processor facilitates addition, deletion and alteration, students can easily experiment with several alternative versions of the text before settling on a final one. Even if, which is unlikely, little discussion surrounds the manipulation of the text, actually doing it will serve to make students aware of how texts can be altered, and what the effects of the alterations are.

**Variation 3:
Using planning
cue cards**

An interesting technique for encouraging students to improve and elaborate their drafts was developed by Carl Bereiter and Marlene Scardamalia (1987), who experimented with using 'planning cues' for various types of essays. The cues given in the two lists below were put on cards, and the writer would, if stuck, select a card from the deck of planning cues, and use it to generate a continuation of the text as if the cue phrase had come to mind spontaneously. Following a demonstration of the procedure by the teacher, students used the cards individually and silently while working on their own writing tasks. To help the students, the cues were grouped into functional categories.

Here are two examples of sets of planning cues, one for opinion essays, the other for factual exposition. You could develop additional sets, together with your students, for other kinds of texts.

*Example 1*

**Planning cues for opinion essays**

**New idea**
An even better idea is . . .
An important point I haven't considered yet is . . .
A better argument would be . . .
A different aspect would be . . .
A whole new way to think of this topic is . . .
No one will have thought of . . .

**Elaborate**
An example of this . . .
This is true, but it's not sufficient so
My own feelings about this are . . .
I'll change this a little by . . .
The reason I think so . . .
Another reason that's good . . .
I could develop this idea by adding . . .
Another way to put it would be . . .
A good point on the other side of the argument is . . .

**Goals**
A goal I think I could write to . . .
My purpose is . . .

### Improve

I'm not being very clear about what I just said so . . .
I could make my main point clear . . .
A criticism I should deal with in my paper is . . .
I really think this isn't necessary because . . .
I'm getting off topic so . . .
This isn't very convincing because . . .
But many readers won't agree that . . .
To liven this up I'll . . .

### Putting it together

If I want to start off with my strongest idea I'll . . .
I can tie this together by . . .
My main point is . . .

*Example 2*

## Planning cues for factual exposition

### New idea

An important distinction is . . .
A consequence of (this is) . . .
The history of this is . . .
Something that is similar is . . .
Its features remind me of . . .
One thing that makes this different from other things like it is . . .
A cause of (this is) . . .
A practical benefit is . . .
A way to improve the use of this is . . .
I might explain a method used to . . .

### Improve

I could describe this in more detail by adding . . .
I could add interest by explaining . . .
This isn't exactly how it is because . . .
I could give the reader a clear picture by . . .
This isn't true of all . . .
To put it more simply . . .
Readers will find it boring to be told . . .

### Elaborate

I'm impressed by . . .
I sometimes wonder . . .
An explanation would be . . .
My own feelings about this are . . .
An example of (this is) . . .
This results in . . .
My own experience with this is . . .

## 5.2.5 Writing a complete text: The mini-saga

If your aim is to have students produce a complete text within a single lesson of fifty minutes, the mini-saga is an admirable choice.

Basically, the mini-saga is a fifty-word story (neither more nor less than fifty words), with up to fifteen additional words for a title. The idea for the mini-saga – which is fast becoming an ELT text-type in its own right – comes from a writing competition organised by the *Daily Telegraph*, in which readers were invited to submit mini-sagas conforming to the above specifications.

As the mini-saga is a total text, the story must be complete, with a beginning, development and conclusion, together with characters and a setting. Thus, it is a kind of novel in miniature. It is an economical way of helping students to come to terms with the organisation of a story. Also, because of the word limit, the writer has to make every word count, which means that it is a good exercise for developing care in the choice of vocabulary and expression.

**Materials**

- Handouts with examples of mini-sagas (see the examples opposite).

**Procedure**

It is a good idea to lead into the mini-saga through the fairy tale, folkstory and fable. Such stories tend to follow much the same pattern, with a situation in which there is a problem that is resolved, leading to the expression of some sort of moral. Because of the virtually universal form of such stories, students of all cultural backgrounds will be able to contribute to the discussion.

1 List on the board a few fairy or folk stories familiar to your students. Ask them to summarise one of the stories and to say what it contains in terms of the following categories:
   – Situation
   – Characters
   – Events
   – Moral

2 Ask students to read a few examples of mini-sagas on the handout, and to comment on them as regards length and text-type. Then tell them that they are going to write a mini-saga which is to be exactly fifty words long, with up to fifteen additional words for a title.

3 When they have finished (after about twenty to thirty minutes), ask students in their groups to read their mini-sagas to each other and to discuss:

   how they discovered their ideas for their mini-saga
   how they developed the story
   how they found a good way of ending it
   what difficulties they had
   how they overcame these difficulties.

   In other words, have a discussion about the process of composing the mini-sagas.

*Examples*

Here are some examples of the range of ideas our students have come up with when asked to write a mini-saga.

---

(a) *Why do they behave so?*
The sheep, the goat and the dog travelled to Legon. Once there the sheep paid his fare, the dog paid more than he should, and the goat paid nothing. Since that day the dog ran after cars, the goat ran from cars but the sheep laid still by the road.

---

(b) *What about the thoughts of the trees?*
I am everywhere, giving you life, in the high mountains, by the powerful sea, in the cities. And you never think about me. I try to talk to you, but you are too busy, too nervous, too unhappy. Please stop and listen to me, I am crying as you are.

---

And here is one of the winning *Daily Telegraph* mini-sagas.

# The postcard

Friendless, he despatched a letter to the twelfth century. Illuminated scrolls arrived by return post. Jottings to Tutankhamun secured hieroglyphs on papyrus; Hannibal sent a campaign report. But when he addressed the future, hoping for cassettes crammed with wonders, a postcard drifted back with scorched edges. It glowed all night.

Variation:
Competition texts

Other possibilities for self-contained texts which could be completed in one lesson come from two writing competitions organised by *The Independent*: a ghost-story of 150 words (see Example 1 overleaf) and a newspaper article of 100 words or less to accompany a headline (see Example 2 overleaf). In addition to the advantages already noted with mini-sages – care over choice of vocabulary and appreciation of text-structure – such competitions will hopefully add an element of fun, humour and word-play to the writing class.

Follow similar procedures as with mini-sagas: discuss the elements we expect in such text-types; provide an example or two to give students an idea of what is required; then ask them to produce a text of their own within the required framework. You could organise a class competition, with students working either individually, or pooling ideas in groups.

*Example 1:*
*Ghost story*

*Example 2:*
*Headliners*

---

*"It's not right," groaned the teenager, "I just don't look old enough for the part". From the darkened hall came a voice. "Perhaps I can help." A figure shuffled into view and the actors saw an old woman with a wrinkled, sagging face. She flicked expertly through the make-up box and in a short while the girl was transformed into an old woman – a carbon copy of its creator.*

*After the performance, the girl could not wait to remove the make-up – it hurt. Cream and then water had no effect. Her screams rent the air. The make-up would not come off – the wrinkles were not greasepaint but living, real. The girl's moans of despair reached the old woman as she smilingly left the theatre – her face smooth and unlined – the face of a girl.*

**Jane Dent**

---

## ABBEY REBELS AIM FOR SEATS ON BOARD

Angry monks are refusing to embark on a 3,000-mile sea crossing to raise money for their abbey because they are expected to stand all the way. Breaking their vow of silence, the rebel monks claim the voyage, a re-creation of a third-century Atlantic crossing, is too hazardous without proper seating. Abbot Billy Benedictus, formerly of Florida Religious Theme Parks Inc., says: "These guys have fallen into bad habits. I've already forbidden socks with sandals and reintroduced hairshirts. The voyage will toughen them. Frankly I don't care if they sit or stand – so long as they keep rowing."

Peter Guttridge

---

**5.2.6 Writing a complete text: Group composition**

Composing together as a group can help to externalise the processes which go on in writing, particularly those concerned with the choices which have to be made at each stage.

**Materials**

- An OHP, OHT acetates (one per group) and OHT pens, or large poster sheets of paper and felt-tip pens.

**Procedure**

1   Have students working in small groups of four or five, and provide each group with an OHT and OHT pen, or poster sheet and felt-tip pen. Use ideas that have been generated in earlier stages as the raw materials for the draft, especially those produced by brainstorming and loopwriting.

2   Tell students to draft out a first version of a text based on these ideas. They will have to discuss not only how they are going to group and structure the ideas, but also the language they will choose to express them. The group secretary writes the text as the group agrees the final form of each sentence.

3   When the drafts are completed, each group displays its draft, either on the OHP or on a wall/board display, and they are evaluated by the class as a whole, using procedures outlined in 6.1 *Assessing the draft* (p. 117). You might also suggest using planning cues to improve the drafts as discussed in 5.2.4 *Variation 3: Using planning cue cards* (p. 110).

If what the groups have written is on OHTs, changes can be written on an overlay (a blank OHT placed on top of the original one). This will show very clearly what the changes are and how they affect the original version. The original draft plus the changes can then be combined in one final version, either on another OHT for further comparison or by each individual student on a paper copy of their own – in which they can, of course, make additional changes as they write if they see fit.

# 6

# Evaluating

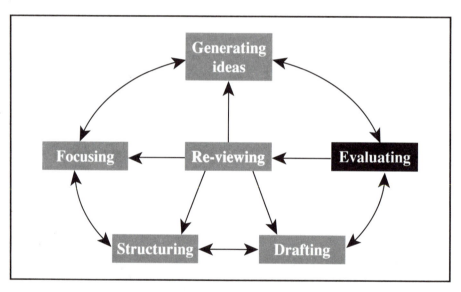

*It is essential that the language be understandable and the reasoning well-maintained . . .*

An area often under-emphasised in the teaching of writing is the cultivation of a sense of responsibility for being one's own critic. Too often students assume that it is their task to write and the teacher's to evaluate.

We believe, however, that our task, as teachers of writing, is in fact a very different one. If, as seems clear, rewriting is what writing is all about – and there are very few of us who get it exactly right first time – we have to try to persuade our students that it is ultimately not the teacher but they themselves who must decide whether their text fulfils its intended goal. They have to be their own evaluators, for without a sense of what is wrong with a text, there is little hope of being able to put it right.

## 6.1 Assessing the draft

The effort that students put into producing a text often has a very limited return in that, not only is it *assessed* only by the teacher, but also *read* only by the teacher. This is neither authentic, in the sense that the writing context is unrepresentative of what happens in the real world, nor is it very productive in helping students develop a sense of good judgement about their writing.

We strongly believe that part of the process of becoming critical about one's writing is getting used to the idea that what you write will be read by many other people. This not only gives you a psychological spur to greater efforts; it also develops your capacity for self-assessment, helping you to become a more observant reader of your own work.

Besides this, though, it is especially helpful to have feedback from other people at the drafting stage, because things which are not clear or which could be improved upon can still be changed. In this sense, writers have some advantage over speakers, who cannot un-make a remark once they have made it. On the other hand, they are at a disadvantage in the sense that once completed, a written record is permanent: readers, unlike listeners, have plenty of opportunity to notice and remember any places where language and presentation are found to be inadequate for any reason. Indeed, readers can choose not to read what the writer offers them, should they find it uninteresting, pointless or incomprehensible.

By learning to evaluate others' writing, and responding in turn to evaluation of their own, students will gradually build up that capacity for self-assessment which is such a vital element in the process of writing.

### 6.1.1 Developing criteria for evaluation

A cognitive approach to writing sees it as a complex series of problem-solving activities. What makes writing so particularly challenging, though, is that writers themselves have to set the right problems to solve. It follows, then, that in order to become a critical reader of one's own work, one first has to have a clear conception of the sorts of things to be critical about.

Students are often under the impression that 'checking one's work' is the equivalent of looking for mistakes – mistakes of spelling, punctuation, grammatical structure, word order and so on. Whilst it is, of course, important (eventually) to see that the text is as error-free as possible, a more fundamental concern which ought to have priority at the drafting stage is the underlying coherence of the writing.

The focus in this activity, then, is for students to consider the sorts of questions writers should ask themselves as they assess how coherently they have presented the information and ideas in their texts. Later, they can apply these questions and general principles of evaluation as they deal with specific problems which arise in their own texts (6.2.2 *Reading and responding: Teacher to class* and 6.2.3 *Reading and responding: Student to student* give further suggestions for developing these skills).

**Materials**

- Handouts of a suitable sample draft text which can be collectively evaluated (numbering the paragraphs and lines will make it easier to refer to the text in discussion – see the example on p. 120).
- If feasible, an OHT of the same draft.
- Text-liners.

**Procedure**

1 Get your students, in groups of two or three, to work together through the text, asking them to mark places where they think the writing is unclear, incomprehensible or capable of being improved. Stress that they should not pay too much attention at this stage to mistakes of spelling, grammar or punctuation unless these interfere with the ideas the writer is trying to convey.

2 Display the same draft text on OHP, and invite suggestions from each group in turn about places where they think it needs to be changed, using an overlay to mark them on the OHT. Add any comments of your own on points which the students may not have covered.

3 Now try to establish why the text is unsatisfactory, and from this discussion compile collectively a list of points to be considered in evaluating the content and presentation of information in a piece of writing. The list should cover the following areas:

---

**Checklist**

(a) Type of writing:
- What type of writing is this text intended to be?
- Does it conform to the conventions usually expected of its type (see 3.4.1 *Comparing charactertistics of text-types* (p. 75)?

(b) Purpose and ideas:
- Is the writer's purpose clear?
- Do we understand the main idea(s)?

(c) Structure of text:
- Is it easy to follow the development of the ideas/argument?
- Would it help to rearrange the sequence of ideas?
- Do the relations between the ideas need to be changed?
- Do the connections between the ideas need to be made more explicit?
- Are the ideas grouped together in a suitable way?
- Is the text segmented into appropriate paragraphs?
- Should any of the paragraphs be joined together?
- Should any of the paragraphs be broken down into smaller units?

(d) Response as readers:
- Does the opening make us want to read on?
- Do we feel satisfied with the way the text comes to an end?
- Are there any points which are not necessary?
- Are there any points which we don't understand?
- Are there any points on which we would like more information?

---

Reproduce this checklist for students to use when they evaluate their own drafts (see 6.1.2 *Becoming your own critic* (p. 121)).

4  As a possible conclusion for this activity, ask the students (in their groups) to redraft the text, bearing in mind the points on the checklist. Copy or display their redrafted versions so that each group sees what the others have done. Discuss which groups have dealt most satisfactorily with the problems originally identified in Step 1 above. Or, if you prefer, redraft the text collectively on the board/OHP.

5  Finally, ask students to supply a title for the text, pointing out that often the best title suggests itself only after the piece is written.

*Example*

Clearly, you will want to choose a draft text which is appropriate for your own students. The *Roundhouse* text (*Figure 29*) is an example of a draft which, though somewhat esoteric in subject matter, has nevertheless proved very successful with many groups of students as a stimulus for starting to be critical. Indeed, precisely because it is esoteric, there is much that needs amending.

We have found it leads to interesting discussions for many reasons, for example:

- the writer's purpose is not clear

- the piece lacks a focus

- there are many options for regrouping ideas and restructuring the text

- the text is not segmented at all, and rather poorly signposted (see 3.4.1 *Comparing characteristics of text-types*, Procedure 1 (p. 75))

- there are many places where elaboration and clarification is required; for instance, the writer never actually tells us what a 'roundhouse' is, nor why it was important to save it

- there is some information which may not be felt to be absolutely essential; for instance, the exact dimensions of the wall, or the folk wisdom about the birds

- there are good examples of how the text fails to conform to conventions of its type; for instance, the use of the P.S. addendum, and abbreviated forms

- there are places where language errors and mechanics need to be edited (though this is not, of course, the main thrust of this particular exercise)

- it is an authentic draft, intended for publication

- it was written by a native speaker of English, and thus drives home the point very effectively that writing is not merely a matter of linguistic proficiency.

Here is the *Roundhouse* text, which was originally meant for publication in a local newsletter. We have glossed information which is not clear, but, of course, if you were to use it with your students, you would probably want to present it to them first without these clarifications.

---

Woodbury Salterton Society[1] were lucky enough to persuaded the developers of Cooke's farm[2] to allow them to to give them the Round House[3] but where to re errect it. Stallcombe House farm[4] came to the rescue. With the help of Man Power Services,
5    Mr Dagworthy[5] & the Devon Rural Skills Trust the Round House was dismantled and transported to Stallcombe. It will be is no easy task reerrecting an ancient building & if it weren't for the skills provided by the Trust and craftsmen it would be impossible. Originally the Round House was attached to a Cob
10    Barn so another cob[6] wall had to be 19' long 2 1/2' thick + 12' high had to be built. A weekend Over 3 weekends A JCB[7] was hired to dig provide clay & over 3 weekends people & bullocks worked to make the cob wall. It is believed this is the 1st cob wall to be built since the turn of early this century. Bullocks
15    trod the clay, oat straw, water & their 'addings' to a cement-like consistency & 3' at a time the wall grew. A It is said a cob wall must start with the nesting of birds & finish when the last had flown. Hidden traditionally In accordance with tradition coins, newspapers – Guardian, Times, Sun & the names of the builders
20    are hidden in the wall. The next exciting stage awaits another weekend. & the next newsletter. *PS* The Devon Rural Skills Trust is a charity Promoting Country Crafts anything from cob walling thatching to making walking sticks. often over a weekend. Skilled craftsmen are paid to teach & pass on arts
25    such as cob walling & thatching that otherwise might be lost for ever.

*Figure 29: Draft 'Roundhouse' text for evaluation*

[1] a society interested in the preservation of the village of Woodbury Salterton
[2] an old farm in the village
[3] a round 19th century building to house a horse-driven treadmill which drove a threshing machine in the barn
[4] a farming community for mentally-handicapped people near the village
[5] a local farmer
[6] traditional building material made of straw and unburned clay
[7] a mechanical digger

In *Figure 30* you will find the redrafted version of this text which actually appeared in the newsletter. You might like to get your students to evaluate how successfully the editor dealt with the problems presented by this draft.

# ROUNDHOUSE GIVEN NEW HOME

Having persuaded the developers of Cooke's Farm not to demolish the mid-19th century Roundhouse there, but to give it to them, Woodbury Salterton Conservation Society had but one problem – where to re-erect it.
Stallcombe House Farm came to the rescue, and with the help of the MSC, farmer Mr. Dagworthy, and the Devon Rural Skills Trust, the Roundhouse was dismantled and transported to Stallcombe.

Re-erecting an ancient building is no easy task, and without the skills offered by the Trust and its craftsmen, the project would not have been feasible. Originally, the Roundhouse (used for housing the horse-powered treadmill for driving the threshing machine in the adjacent barn) was attached to a cob-built barn. A cob wall, therefore, has had to be built at Stallcombe to accommodate the new guest. To construct this wall (19' x 12' x 2.5'), a JCB digger was hired to provide the clay, and over the course of 3 weekends volunteer humans and commandeered bullocks laboured together to start the process – the first time, incidentally, that a cob wall is believed to have been built in this area since early in the century.

Bullocks trod the clay, oat straw, water and their own 'additions' – an essential ingredient, this, for a good cob wall – into a cement-like consistency, and gradually the wall took shape, 2 feet at a time. It is said that a cob wall must start with the nesting of birds and finish when the last has flown. If this timetable was not strictly adhered to in this case, at least the tradition of hiding coins, newspapers and the names of the builders in the wall was very carefully observed. The next exciting stage of this project awaits another weekend – and a report of it, the next edition of 'Stallcombe News'. Incidentally, the Devon Rural Skills Trust is a charity set up to preserve ancient country crafts, ranging from cob-walling and thatching to making walking sticks. Skilled craftsmen are paid to teach and pass on such arts which might otherwise be lost for ever. Perhaps Stallcombe might be able, at some future date, to offer a home to some of these skills, and workshop space to their practitioners – a possible new lease of life for the Roundhouse itself, perhaps?

*Figure 30: Reformulated 'Roundhouse' text*

## 6.1.2 Becoming your own critic

The focus here is on putting into practice the principles developed in 6.1.1 *Developing criteria for evaluation* (p. 117), whereby students apply the evaluation criteria to their own and other students' work. Since the principles remain the same regardless of what is being evaluated, this activity can be used with any draft texts which the students produce.

| **Materials** | • Copies of the students' draft texts (if possible, number the paragraphs and lines before you copy them for ease of reference later). |
| | • Handouts of an 'evaluation checklist', compiled from points discussed in 6.1.1 *Developing criteria for evaluation* (see *Figure 31*). |
| | • Text-liners. |

**Procedure**

We leave the finer details of organising this activity to you, the individual teacher, since how you decide to carry it out will depend very much on factors such as the size of your class, the availability of copying facilities and how well your students know each other. We have found it to work successfully with students grouped in threes.

The general principle is to get the students to read critically first their own draft, and then the draft(s) of one or more of the other students. They should use an evaluation checklist – along the lines of that in *Figure 31* – to help them, noting down their observations about each text and highlighting places which need to be amended or changed.

Later, the members of the group discuss each of their texts in turn, pooling their suggestions for improvement. This discussion provides the basis for a second, individually written draft.

An alternative way of approaching this kind of evaluation task is given in 6.2.2 *Reading and responding: Teacher to class* (p. 128), where you will find a detailed analysis of one particular draft text as an example. And in 6.2.3 *Reading and responding: Student to student* (p. 130), there are further suggestions for ways of getting students to respond to each other's texts.

**Variation:
Listening to
recorded drafts**

Since it is often difficult to be objective about one's own writing, having the draft read aloud by someone else and listening to it without reference to the written version may help writers become aware of problems they did not notice whilst writing their draft or reading it over.

You will need tape-recorders (or you could use the language lab) for this variation, where students, instead of simply reading each other's drafts, record them as they read them aloud. Have the students working in groups of three or four, with one tape-recorder per group, if possible. Alternatively, the task can be done simply by having students read each other's work aloud, although we have found this to be less motivating. Another option is to have students working in pairs in the language lab.

A member of the group reads aloud someone else's draft text. When all the texts have been recorded, the tape is played back and, without looking at the written texts, students identify points where the texts are not satisfactory. The discussion provides a basis for redrafting.

If students work in the language lab, get each student to read and record their partner's draft text and then to exchange recordings. They listen to their text being read, without looking at the written version, and discuss the improvements they think need to be made both to their own and their partner's text.

| | Text A | Text B | Text C |
|---|---|---|---|
| **Form**<br><br>1  What type of writing is this supposed to be?<br><br>2  Has writer observed conventions expected of this type of writing? | | | |
| **Purpose and ideas**<br><br>3  Is the purpose clear? What is it?<br><br>4  Are the main ideas clear? What are they? | | | |
| **Structure of text**<br><br>5  Do relations between ideas need to be made clearer? Where?<br><br>6  Do ideas need to be resequenced? How?<br><br>7  Is text segmented into suitable paragraphs? If not, where is adjustment needed? | | | |
| **Response as reader**<br><br>8  Is beginning suitable? If not, why?<br><br>9  Is ending suitable? If not, why?<br><br>10  Any points unnecessary? Which?<br><br>11  Any points need to be clarified? Which?<br><br>12  Any points need to be expanded? Which? | | | |

*Figure 31: Content evaluation checklist*

## 6.2 Responding

In a process approach, reading students' work involves responding to the text as a *reader*, rather than simply as a *marker*. Even if, eventually, the linguistic, stylistic or formal features of the text are evaluated, the first reading should be concerned with meaning and purpose. Doing this requires the exercise of some self-control on the part of teachers more used to reacting to a text as a piece of language.

Obviously, some tact and sensitivity is needed when entering into this new relationship with the writer. So, the teacher-cum-reader must be supportive and helpful in the kinds of comments that are made, accentuating the positive rather than focusing on the negative aspects of what the student has presented.

The activities outlined in 6.1 *Assessing the draft* (pp. 117–123) make clear our belief that *students* should also read and respond to each other's work. For it is important that they acquire the habit of judging a text in terms of its meaning for them, and of considering what the writer would need to do to make the text as comprehensible as possible for them as readers. By turning the tables in this way, students will be helped to understand the crucial point that writers write for readers, and that effective writing is influenced by this knowledge. Even when writers are writing for themselves, they are still writing for a reader, in this case the same person as the writer. We all have the experience of having written something for ourselves which, on subsequent reading, is ambiguous or opaque.

Writing which is to be published has to meet even more stringent demands, even when students are writing for each other. 'Publishing' student work, in the sense of 'making it public', whilst not necessarily involving printing and distributing as in the case of a newspaper or book, can help to motivate students by giving them an audience; at the same time, the reading and discussion of each others' work entailed also helps to foster a sense of judgement.

The activities which follow involve three kinds of responding. The first is a personal and individual response by the teacher to the student writer. The second is a public response by the teacher to the work of one student as a whole class activity. The third involves students responding to each other's work.

**6.2.1 ▶**
**Reading and responding: Teacher to student**

As readers, we have to respond to rather than merely assess our students' writing. And though we may not ostensibly be concerned with the language at this point, one of the virtues of the 'draft-respond-redraft-respond-redraft' sequence is that often the language of the product as well as its overall coherence and effectiveness improves as the students try to express their thoughts more clearly and appropriately. A good illustration of this can be found in Mitsuo Toki's texts in the *Introduction* (*Figure 2*). Some examples of teachers' responses to students' texts will illustrate what is involved in the responding process.

**Materials**

● Students' own texts.

**Procedure**

Read the texts in question, and record your responses to them in writing. The students then use these comments as a basis for redrafting, or you can use them as a starting point for an individual conference with each student (see 6.3.1 *Continuing and improving the draft* (p. 131).

We find the notes of Frank Diffley and Ronald Lapp (1988) on written feedback a useful guideline for teacher response to students' work. They are as follows:

- Respond in pencil or black ink. Red pens can be threatening.
- Write comments and notes in the margins and avoid comments which correct spelling, grammar and mechanics.
- All comments should be specific and content-related. Avoid comments which can apply to any text.
- Reread your responses and ask yourself if they make sense.
- Ask students for feedback on the responses given to them.
- Respond as a genuine and interested reader rather than as a judge and evaluator ('We should respond not so much to student writing but to student writers.' (Vivian Zamel 1985))

*Example 1*

In this example, the task was 'divergent' or open-ended, in that the students had been encouraged to write about the topic – *Family New Year celebrations in your country* (a Cambridge First Certificate topic) – from their own point of view rather than attempting to 'converge' towards any prescribed model in terms of ideas and organisation.

On receiving the students' first drafts, the teacher wrote individual comments in the form of a letter. Here is one student's draft, and the teacher's response to it.

**Gabrielle's first draft**

---

Family celebrations in my country at New Year is very important. They usually, on 31st of December stay until 12:00 o'clock in midnight to wait for New Year and then they visit friends. The meaning of that day for me is that you start a new year with new expectations for the future. You hope that it could be the best year for yourself.

Apart from that, you hope to have a great success in your work or in your studies.

On the other hand, people in Uruguay, use to send greeting cards to their friends and relative (parents, cousins, uncles, nephew, etc.)

However some families get together for that day, I mean grandparents, parents, brothers, sisters, and children. There are some that don't get the custom to join together.

Uruguayans usually have a special dinner. They eat things like pig, like barbecue, veal and kind of salad for example, mixed salad (lettuce and tomatoes) or a russia salad (potatoes, carrots, peas). they drink any kind of drinks, from coke to wine. There are lot of Uruguayans that get drunk on New Year, specially young people.

On the other hand, the people use to buy bombas and fireworks and all those sort of things. So then, they through the bombas and the fuegos artificiales at the midnight of 31st December. And it is like a explosion everywhere and you look to the dark sky and it seems like a special party. Everywhere there are lights and some things like that.

People go to bed late in the night on 31st December because as you know here in Uruguay is sumer in New Year and so everyone go outside and dance in the streets. Everyone is happy.

---

**Teacher's response**

---

Dear Gabrielle,

I really enjoyed reading your draft. You have some good expressions, e.g.

*. . . you look to the dark sky and it seems like a special party.*

Why don't you begin with that sentence? e.g.

*I looked up at the dark sky and it seemed like a special party. It was like an explosion everywhere. People were throwing fireworks into the sky, and everywhere there were lights.*

Now, at this point you can tell your reader what night it is:

*It was New Year's Eve, and everyone was celebrating.*

Then you can explain what New Year's Eve means in Uruguay, how families and friends come together and how everyone has hopes for the future. You can end by coming back to the idea of fireworks.

You can organise your essay to have two times:

| | | |
|---|---|---|
| Past | *I looked up . . .*<br>*it seemed . . .* | Introduction |
| General<br>present | *Family celebrations in*<br>*Uruguay are very*<br>*important.*<br>*People usually send*<br>*greetings to each other . . .* | Body |
| Past | *????* | Conclusion |

---

*Example 2*   This example is a composition written by an Indonesian student in a teachers' college on the topic *My most unforgettable character*. What may have started out for most of the students in the group as another tedious writing assignment seemed, for many, to become an essay in self-knowledge and self-disclosure. That it did so points to the need for trust between teacher and learner, and for tact on the part of the teacher in responding to the text.

Virtually all of the writing was, by conventional standards, somewhat sentimental, but it is this very characteristic which engages the reader; the writers had become caught up by and committed to their subject.

Here is the student's essay, and some of the responses made by the teacher to the writer, beginning with an enthusiastic reaction to the story.

### My most unforgettable character

In our life, of course we have experiences or impressions. Whether they are good or bad. Sometimes they are caused of someone's action or come from ourselves so that we cannot forget them forever. As human being who live in society I also have an experience that makes me difficult to forget it. An impressive experience that gave by a girl that I knew as a nurse at public hospital in this town.

At the end of the year 1982 I had an traffic accident on Jalan Veteran. The accident made my leg broken so that I had to stay for a few months at the hospital. Here, in the hospital was the first time I met the girl.

In a morning when I woke up, a girl with white dress stood beside my bed while greeting me 'good morning'. Being aware that there was somebody greeted me, I then looked to the coming sound. The fact was that the sound came from the girl that I knew her name was 'Nellimurni' the nurse. She was 20 years old, 160 centimetres tall. She has round face and beautiful and wore classes. Her white and tidy arranged teeth added her beauty when she smiled. These gave me impression that she as a friendly girl. The fact was like that. Because as long as I stayed at the hospital she always help me whether in the morning or in the afternoon. Even if she did not work she also visit me in my room. Sometimes she brings me fruits, bread, milk, etc. When I noticed her admiringly, she broke my imagination by asking me whether I want to take a bath or wash the face. After thinking about it then I made up my mind just to wash my face and clean my body. Fastly, she prepared everything to help me. After she take care of me she also clean my bed. Before she leave my room I asked her whether she likes to help me next time. Infact, she made up her mind that she was ready to help me as long as I stayed at the hospital. I felt happy that there somebody who like helping me, although I knew that her duty as nurse was taking care of patient. But, for me, her helps was a special attention, because at a public hospital it was rare to find a nurse who want to take care her patient as given to me except if we stayed at V.I.P. room with good facilities.

But, since this last one year I never meet her. I heard from her friends that she moved to Bandung to continue her study. I felt disappointed that she did not tell me when she will move. I lost a friend who had unforgettable characters. Although she had weaknesses, I always remember her. Once, one day I refused her gift. She became angry with me. She did not want to talk with me for a few days. After I explained what happened with me she began understand me. However, she was my most unforgettable character in my life.

**Teacher's notes**

---

1 I really appreciate your sharing this experience with me. I found your story to be a touching piece of writing.

2 The first two paragraphs could be made more interesting for the reader. How?

3 Try changing the order of events and paragraphs. For instance, you could begin like this:

*In the morning, when I woke up, she stood by my bed. Wearing a white dress, she greeted me, 'Good morning.' I looked around to find the person who was speaking to me. It was Nellimurni, the nurse.*

Or you could begin with your second paragraph.

4 Why is such an opening more interesting for the reader?

5 What other changes will you make if you begin like this?

---

**6.2.2 Reading and responding: Teacher to class**

Although, ideally, each student will receive individual attention and response from the teacher, there are occasions when this is not feasible and it is then that the work of one or two students can be dealt with publicly. While such a procedure may be more time-efficient, it has its limitations and some tact may be needed to avoid mortifying the student whose work has been chosen for public scrutiny. However, if the students know each other quite well, we have found that they eventually come to appreciate – and perhaps even to enjoy – having their work pulled to pieces.

**Materials**

- Handout A: a sample student text.
- Handout B: sections of the text displayed under rhetorical categories: generalisation, example, etc.
- Handout C: a reformulated version of the text, if desired.
  (If possible, have all these handouts on OHT as well.)
- Text-liners.

**Procedure**

To illustrate the procedure, a short essay written by an Iraqi student attending a pre-sessional course at a British university will be used as the focus text. The class had been given the topic *Cats as domestic animals*, and the focus in this particular writing class was on organising an argument. You would, of course, have to adapt the procedure given below if you wanted to focus on a different text-type or another aspect of the writing.

Use the text either as it is (see Example: A), or in a version which is corrected for grammatical and mechanical errors (see Example: B). The advantage of using such a corrected version is that student attention will not be diverted to surface errors at this stage. The disadvantage is that time and opportunity will have to be found to make and copy a typed version. However, if the text is brief, this is not a major problem.

1 Display, or distribute copies of, the focus text. Ask students first to break up the text into sections according to the way the argument is presented, and then to distinguish between general statements and examples. These can be underlined with text-liners on copies given to the students and on the OHT version (Handout A). Then display these different parts of the text on a separate OHT (Handout B), for instance:

**Generalisations**
Cats are useless as domestic animals.
In cities there is no problem with rats and mice.

**Examples**
I haven't kept a cat.
My brother has a son, and he had a cat.

2 Ask students to distinguish between points in favour of cats and points against cats as domestic animals, for instance:

| For | Against |
| --- | --- |
| Pets for children | Death can cause unhappiness |
| They catch rats and mice | Rats and mice aren't a problem in most towns and cities |

3 Ask students to suggest what the writer has not made explicit, e.g. the relationship between cats as rodent catchers and the claim that rats and mice aren't a problem in towns and cities.

4 Ask students to suggest how a reorganisation of ideas would make the text better. Basically, the writer is presenting points for and against keeping cats as domestic pets, but his organisation of these points is not very clear to the reader. How could the organisation be made more explicit? Note also the importance of providing a clear introduction to the argument and a clear conclusion. Discuss ways in which these could be expressed.

5 Ask students to rewrite the focus text and compare their rewritten versions for organisation and clarity.

6 Display or distribute a reformulated version of the text if you wish (Handout C) and compare it both with the original and with versions produced by the students (see Example: C).

*Example*          **A: Original version**

> The cats are useless
>
> The cats ~~are~~ (is) useless as domesic animal. Specially in cities where is no problem of rates and mices, In my life, ~~the~~ (I haven't) kept a cat in the house, I think, ~~this~~ decision come from that of my life is full of hard work. Perhaps, you might say, It is a nice thing to find a game (cat) for your children, as domastic animal. I reply, OK, ~~for~~ I before like ~~that~~ thing one time a week while I don't ~~she~~ leave my children to play with useless game. My brother has a son, and His (had) ~~and kept his~~ a cat, later on, the cat was died. However The boy was in deep sorrow and still of this feeling for a long time.

### B: Corrected version

Cats are useless as domestic animals. Especially in cities, there is no problem of rats and mice. In all my life I haven't kept a cat in the house. I think this decision comes from the fact that my life is full of hard work. Perhaps you might say: It is a nice thing to find a plaything for young children, such as a domestic animal. I reply: OK, I like things once a week, but I don't let my children play with useless playthings. My brother has a son. He had a cat. Later the cat died. The boy was in deep sorrow and remained so for a long time.

### C: Reformulated version

Various arguments are put forward by people in support of cats as domestic animals. Some say that they can be playthings for children, though I think that we could give children more useful playthings. But cats can also cause children unhappiness. My brother, for example, has a son. This boy had a cat which he loved. The cat died and the boy was very depressed for a long time. I think this was bad.

Other people say that cats are useful because they destroy rats and mice, but I don't see that this is a good argument in modern cities where there is no problem of rats and mice.

In conclusion, I think cats are useless as domestic animals and I myself have never kept a cat in my life.

## 6.2.3 Reading and responding: Student to student

There is some overlap here with the evaluation procedure outlined in 6.1.2 *Becoming your own critic* (p. 117). However, whereas in 6.1.2 the stress is on becoming objective about one's own writing, here the focus is on how we respond to others' texts as readers.

**Materials**

- Students' own draft texts.

**Procedure**

1 Have students work with a partner, and get each to read what the other has drafted so far. They should make notes of places in their partner's draft:
   - that they particularly liked or enjoyed
   - that they particularly disliked or found unnecessary
   - that they found unclear
   - that they would have liked to know more about.
   Lastly they should summarise their partner's text: *The main idea in this paper is . . .*
2 They now return their papers to each other and discuss the summary and the points that they have noted, beginning with the good points and going on to the things that need clarifying or improving. In the process, they should try jointly to improve what they have written.

   As suggested in the *Introduction* (p. 10), you may like to experiment with the occasional inter-class exchange of texts. Though it may not be feasible on a regular basis, we have found it stimulating as an exercise in student-student responding.

*Example*

Here is a fellow student's response to the text of Gabrielle, the Uruguayan student whose essay is to be found above in 6.2.1 (p. 124). This was her first attempt at writing a response to a text, and as you will see, there is room for improvement. However, it is a start in the right direction.

> I like very much Gabrielle's writing the part in which she talked about the fire works. It is marvelous thinking about a dark sky plenty of lights. The paper is about Uruguayan's customs in New Year celebration. The main idea is it has is that the family get together to share a special dinner and to have a very happy celebration.

## 6.3 Conferencing

Conferencing is a procedure in which the teacher/reader or another reader (such as a fellow student) and the writer work together on what the writer has written, motivated by a concern with clarifying the writer's intentions, purpose and meanings. Conferencing can be carried out either during or after composition and it has the virtue of enabling the teacher to give individual attention to each student so that better advice can be provided than is generally possible with written remarks. Furthermore, conferencing is conducted on a face-to-face basis, so that students can respond to the reader's questions and comments as well as adding their own. The discussion can be one of joint negotiation of meaning, whereas written comments tend to be one-way.

As regards continuing a draft once begun, there is no simple, mechanical way of doing this because the process of drafting, like the complete process of writing itself, is more organic than mechanical, more recursive than linear. If students have already engaged in the type of activities described in 2 *Generating* (pp. 17–43) and 3 *Focusing* (pp. 44–77), they should have plenty of ideas and a quantity of notes. They may also have a plan, either in their heads or on paper, to guide the development of their draft. What they now need during the drafting stage will be reminders to refer back to their notes, keeping in mind their thesis and viewpoint and the reader's interests and attitudes. Conferencing is a very effective way of drawing the students' attention to such matters.

**6.3.1 ▶**
**Continuing and improving the draft**

You will probably find that you develop your own approach to conferencing, the conduct of which, being face-to-face interaction, will naturally depend on the personalities of the teacher and student concerned. What we suggest is that you look through the following two sets of ideas for an effective conferencing session, gleaning from them strategies which you think you could use with your own students.

**Procedure**

1   The first set of ideas comes from Donald Graves (1983), whose work with young children in the native English-speaking writing class has been very influential, both with regard to process approaches to writing in general, and to the technique of conferencing in particular.

He has suggested the following questions as a basis for a teacher/student conference:

### Before writing

1 What are you going to be writing about? (Topic choice is free.)
2 How are you going to put that down on paper?
3 How did you go about choosing your subject?
4 What problems might you run into?

### While writing

1 How is it going?
2 What are you writing about now?
3 Where are you now in your draft?
4 I noticed that you changed your lead. It is much more direct. How did you do that?
5 If you are about to put new information in here, how would you go about doing it?
6 When you don't know how to spell a word, how do you go about figuring what to do?
7 What strategy do you use for figuring out where one sentence ends and the other begins?
8 What will you do with this piece of writing when it is all done?

### After writing

1 How did you go about this?
2 Did you make any changes?
3 What are you going to do next with this piece of writing?
4 What do you think of this piece of writing?

Graves also suggests that the teacher should sit next to and not opposite the writer, so as to avoid an adversarial posture, and that time must be allowed for the student to answer. He suggests allowing for pauses of at least fifteen seconds between a question and answer.

Finally, it is a good idea to read through the text silently with the student before beginning the conference. This ensures that both student and teacher are familiar with the text when they start to discuss it

2 The second set of ideas comes from Frank Diffley and Ronald Lapp (1988), working with adult ESL students with limited literacy skills in English.

1 Help the student to relax. Make the situation non-threatening by finding something to praise.
2 Interact with the student. Establish a collaborative relationship.
3 Engage the student in the analysis process. Give every opportunity for the student to do the talking and make the revision decisions.
4 Attend to global problems before working on sentence and word level problems.
5 Respond to the writing as work in progress or under construction.
6 Ask the students to sum up the changes they need to make for revision.
7 End the conferencing session with praise and encouragement.

They also give some other points for consideration.

1 Converse with the student. Listen to what the student has to say. Allow the student to originate and take credit for ideas.
2 Give advice which is specific and relevant so that the student will understand the need to revise as well as how to revise.
3 Serve as a model writer. Talk about work that you are writing and revising. Students need to understand that native speakers revise and rewrite extensively.
4 Make responses text-specific rather than using vague comments which can refer equally well to other texts. Offer specific strategies, questions and suggestions which help students revise and reshape their texts. Avoid contradiction.
5 View yourself as a *writing* teacher rather than a *language* teacher, because when attending to language problems, meaning and associated global problems are often ignored.

**6.3.2 ►**
**Responding to student self-evaluation**

Conferencing can be combined with various forms of student self-evaluation, in which students annotate their own texts at points about which they are uncertain, where they would like the teacher's advice.

One method of doing this, developed by Maggie Charles (1988), is for students to put numbers in their draft texts at points where they would like some help, and write the corresponding question or comment either in a column alongside their text, or at the end, as in Example 1 below. As Charles points out, and as experience in using the technique has revealed, what the students think is important is not necessarily the same as what the teacher considers important. What is needed, therefore, is a period of training in which the students gradually increase the sophistication of their self-evaluation, and move from paying most attention to surface features of the text to realising that there are more fundamental aspects of organisation and meaning which need improving.

Another scheme, suggested by Norman Coe (1989), is more focused, and has the additional virtue of making students more independent in that *they* tell the teacher the kind of help they want. Here students use the following code, which they put in the margin at appropriate places in their text, rather like a teacher's marking code. The difference is that in this case, the code is there for the teacher to use as a guide to the areas in which the student wants help:

**R**      Please reply to content.
**CM**    Please correct mistakes.
**IM**     Please indicate (but don't correct) mistakes.
**IMAC** Indicate mistakes and add category (e.g. V for verb error, T for tense, etc.).
**WUO** Comment on words underlined only. (In this case, the student may be trying something out and may not be sure whether it is acceptable, appropriate or correct. The underlining of words or sections concerned encourages students to experiment and show that they are doing so.)

**Materials**
- Students' own writing, with their own annotations.

**Procedure**

1 Explain to your students that you want them to tell you what points they wish to have advice on. To do this, they should annotate their texts using either of the schemes mentioned on p. 133. To make sure they understand the idea, you can show the students Example 1 below, and work through some of the points which the writer has referred to.

2 Tell students to annotate their own drafts, and discuss the points in the students' annotations when they come to you for a conference.

*Example 1:*
*Conference with*
*Angelina*

Here is part of a conference with Angelina, a Uruguayan student writing about New Year festivities (see also 6.2.1 *Reading and responding: Teacher to student* (p. 124)) in which the numbered points she herself had raised in her self-evaluation are being discussed ((1) and (2) below). First, part of her second draft is given, followed by a transcript of the related portion of the conference.

**Excerpt from Angelina's second draft**

> Is a nice day, the families get together and have dinner on 31st December and have lunch on 1st January. The families (1) get together about nine or ten o'clock in the night, have a special dinner, with meats, salads and so on. Then we usually go to a pub or to other house to celebrate the New year dancing and singing. We met our friends we go to other houses and congratulate each other. We usually go to bed very late. We were very tired· for dancing and drinks, so (2) 1st January we get up late and the cities are very quiet. We got together again to have lunch, and we continue regarding friends and neighbours, we eat the same kind of food.
> (1) repeat vocabulary
> (2) is this expression correct?

**Extract from conference with Angelina**

TEACHER: (reading) The families (1) *get together* about nine. Why not just *meet*? What's the next one?

ANGELINA: Here. So, (2) *first January* or *January first*?

TEACHER: Why not say, *so on New Year's day*? That's correct so far. It should be *so on New Year's day*. Why not say, *so on New Year's day we get up late. We get together again . . . meet* or . . . *assemble* is another word we could use.

ANGELINA: *We, we, we . . .* all the time *we.*

TEACHER: Well, you could say *everyone, all of us.* You must make sure you've got a subject in all your sentences. What's the next one? . . .

*Example 2: Gabrielle's final draft*

After two drafts and the kinds of feedback and discussion described in this section and in 6.2.1, *Reading and responding: Teacher to student*, Gabrielle, the Uruguayan student whose first *New Year* draft appears in 6.2.1, produced a third and final version which, while not perfect, indicates the benefits of the work which had gone into it.

---

**Special day**

I looked up at the dark sky and it seemed like a special party. It was like an explosion everywhere. People were throwing fireworks into the sky and everywhere there were lights. It was New Year's eve, and everyone was celebrating.

Family celebrations in Uruguay are very important. Families get together and have special dinner for that day with their children and grandparents. They usually visit their friends and neighbours and greet them, after New Year's eve. Everyone is happy. There are special dances that they have in the streets and old people, middle-aged and very young go to those dances. Moreover, discoteques organise special parties for New Year and arrange the discoteque for that day with some special things. As well as, people usually send greeting cards to each other.

Another thing that you must remember is that here, in New Year is summer and students are in their summer vacation. However, workers haven't got a special vacation for New Year. They try to take some days free for New Year's eve.

I remember last New Year when all were waiting for it and I was in the garden with my dog and it barked and ran into the house. I didn't know why but when I looked to the sky and heard the noises of the bombas that the children were throwing I understood the reason of its fear: the party started in the sky and I could see lights everywhere. New Year has come.

---

# 7

# Re-viewing

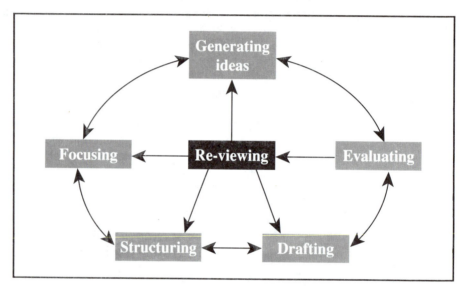

*Inspect your soldiers from the rear rank to the front, down to the minutest detail, decide on retaining or rejecting by the turn of a hair . . .*

As writers work on shaping their ideas through various processes of focusing, structuring, drafting, evaluating and redrafting, their texts gradually evolve into a form which is more or less final. They will already have made most of their major decisions about which words and structures best give expression to their ideas.

One essential part of the process remains, though, namely to 're-view' the text, as if with a new pair of eyes. And often, even at this stage, a new look at what is on the page is quite likely to give rise to yet more ideas and thoughts which have to be worked into the original conception. Indeed, there is a sense in which a writing task never ends; instead, we simply have to decide that we have reached the point where we must abandon our text to its fate.

Whereas the re-viewing process requires a sense of judgement – an awareness that all is not quite right with the text – the actual amending process requires adequate linguistic tools to work with. All the activities in this section, therefore, have a dual objective: to further develop critical capacities, and at the same time to enrich the repertoire of linguistic resources which are the essential tools for writing. The tasks suggested can be used as extensions of work done in any of the previous sections, or, indeed, they can be applied to any written text produced by students.

## 7.1 Checking the context

In earlier sections (see 3.2 *Considering purpose*, 3.3 *Considering audience* and 3.4 *Considering form* in particular) we discussed at some length why it is necessary for writers to get to grips with the *context* of the piece they are writing: its purpose, audience and form. In this activity, the focus is on an overall assessment of the text to check how successful the writer has been in taking these three contextual factors into account.

Try to preserve an element of anonymity by having the texts which the students are to assess typed, or printed out on the word processor. Not only does this make the task more intriguing; it also lessens the risk of subjective judgements.

**Materials**

- One copy of a final draft of a text from each student (typed/printed out and anonymous). The texts should be roughly the same length, but not all of the same type. You could select suitable drafts from each student's work over a period of time, or ask students to supply a favourite text they have written, or use a selection of texts produced as the outcome of the activity suggested in 3.4.2 *Varying the form*. Gather the drafts in before the class, and assign to each a number or letter for later reference.
- 'Context' checklists for all the students (see *Figure 32*).

**Procedure**

1 Explain to your students that the object of this re-viewing session is to read the texts and assess what the *context* of each text was supposed to be. Provide checklists along the lines of that in *Figure 32* below for them to make notes as they read. (It would be helpful for the students to have made a note for themselves of what the context of their own text is before beginning the reviewing procedure.)

2 Have the texts in a central file. The students each take a text from the file, read it and note their comments on their checklist. They return this text to the file when they have finished with it, take a new one and repeat the procedure for as long as time permits and interest is maintained. Each student should aim to evaluate at least three or four texts. *Make sure that students note the numbers of the texts they read.* Warn them that if they pick their own text, they should treat it exactly as the others, trying to be as objective as possible about it.

3 Now ask someone to start the discussion by reading out the notes they have made on one of the texts. The other students who have read that particular text should add their comments and opinions. The objective is, of course, to see how closely the notes of the readers tally with the original intentions of the writer of the text in question.

If there are discrepancies, discuss how the writer might amend the text, by adding more information, rearranging the sequence of ideas, changing the style, and so on.

4 Repeat this procedure until all the drafts have been discussed. Obviously, if the class is large, this will become boring, in which case you could get the students to work from the start in smaller groups, reading only the texts of those in their group. Alternatively, use texts which the students have produced from groupwork, in which case the evaluation is also done on a group basis, thus reducing the time needed to get through all the texts.

| Text | Purpose of text | Possible audience | Type of writing |
|------|------------------|--------------------|------------------|
|      |                  |                    |                  |

*Figure 32 'Writing context' checklist*

## 7.2 Checking connections

All writing, no matter how humble, is consciously created, and results from complex cognitive processes involving translation of non-linear thought into linear written language. Of course, some kinds of writing are clearly more spontaneous than others: a note left for a friend who was out when you called to visit, for instance, will obviously require far less conscious effort to write than will an academic paper written for a degree supervisor. Yet no written text is an entirely random collection of words and information. The writer inevitably imposes some sort of order upon the various elements which make up the text, and is therefore responsible for making sure that the connections – both logical and linguistic – between these elements have been made clear to the reader.

## 7.2.1 Testing logical links

To translate amorphous thought into structured language successfully, we have to make sure that the train of thought which is perfectly clear to us *in our head* is equally clear to the reader *on the page*. The focus in this unit is on:

a) testing out whether logical links between ideas are clear
b) considering linguistic devices available to writers to make logical connections clear to readers.

## Materials

- Handouts of a 'logical connectives chart' (see Step 1 below, and *Figure 33*).
- A suitable sample draft text (as in 6.1.1 *Developing criteria for evaluation, Figure 29* (p. 120) or 6.2.2 *Reading and responding: Teacher to class* Example (p. 129)), both on OHT and as a handout for your students.
- Handouts of a fairly short text in final version, suitable for the level and interests of your students.
- Students' own final version texts.
- Red pens.

## Procedure

1 Start off with the students in small groups, and get them to brainstorm for a few minutes as many connective expressions as they can think of within the four basic logical categories: *and, or, but* and *for* (meaning *because*).

2 Ask each group in turn to suggest expressions for each category, for example:

| **and** | **or** | **but** | **for** |
|---|---|---|---|
| moreover | alternatively | however | since |
| furthermore | on the other hand | although | because |
| first . . . second | | by contrast | |
| equally | | | |

Write them on the OHP/board, until all suggestions are exhausted. Then distribute handouts of the 'logical connectives chart' (see *Figure 33*) and suggest to your students that they could build up for themselves a stock of further examples of logical connectives (together with a note of their usual positions in a sentence or clause) as they come across them in their reading.

3 Now ask the students to regroup into twos or threes and get them to work on the sample draft text. They should disregard the fact that the ideas may not be in a good order or that the information needs clarifying, but should consider the draft 'as is'.

Ask them to think about the logical connections between each idea and – preferably with a red pen, or anything which will stand out clearly – to annotate the text with a suitable expression, using the chart compiled in Step 2 above to help them.

Or, they may find that an easier way to do this is by asking and answering questions about how the ideas are connected (as in Example 1).

If the connecting ideas are *implicit* in the text, they should try to make them *explicit* in their own words. The idea is to lay bare the train of thought which produced the text, and to understand the connections between each item of information.

4  Display the OHT of the same sample draft text, and, in a whole class discussion, annotate it according to the students' suggestions. (Use an overlay to do this.)

Then discuss whether there are any places where the connections between the ideas which have been made explicit can be left implicit and yet still be understood.

In the light of this discussion about the train of thought underlying the draft text, decide whether the ideas need to be rearranged. If so, discuss various options for a new structure, and decide whether any additional logical linking expressions are required.

5  So far the students have been working with a text which is not in its final version. Get them now to work with a suitable final version text, and – although it may at first seem a strange operation – ask them to repeat the procedures of Step 3 above to understand the train of thought underlying the words on the page (see Example 1).

In a whole class discussion, draw attention to:
(a)  how the logical links between the items often remain implicit, and how they often depend on knowledge of the world shared between writer and reader (otherwise the text would become incomprehensibly unwieldy)
(b)  how writers sometimes use certain punctuation symbols (such as colons or dashes) to indicate logical connections
(c)  the position of linking expressions in the sentences. Point out that the position of some linking devices can vary (e.g. *whereas* can be used both at the beginning and in the middle of a sentence), but that others are usually used in a fixed position (e.g. *too* goes at the end of a sentence, clause or phrase).

6  Finally, extend the discussion to the students' own texts. Ask them to exchange texts with a partner, and mark the places where they consider the logical links between the ideas to be either wrong, inadequate, missing or superfluous (see Example 2).

They then discuss each other's work, and suggest ways of improving the drafts. Your function at this stage is to circulate, giving advice and help where necessary.

(Based on Quirk *et. al.*, 1972: Chapter 10.17 – 10.38)

| | | |
|---|---|---|
| and | Listing<br>Cataloguing<br>e.g. *First, . . .*<br>   *Another . . .*<br>   *Finally, . . .* | Adding to what has gone before<br>Reinforcing<br>e.g. *Also*        Equating<br>   *Moreover, . . .*   e.g. *. . . too*<br>   *Furthermore, . . .*      *Equally . . .* |

| | |
|---|---|
| | Transition, leading to a new stage in sequence, or digression<br>e.g. *As for . . .*<br>   *With reference to . . .*<br>   *Incidentally, . . .* |
| | Summing up what has gone before<br>e.g. *In short, . . .*<br>   *Briefly, . . .* |
| | Referring backwards or forwards to similar ideas/references<br>e.g. *That is to say, . . .*<br>   *For example, . . .* |
| | Expressing results or consequences<br>e.g. *Therefore, . . .*<br>   *Accordingly, . . .* |
| | Inferring from a previous statement<br>e.g. *In other words, . . .*<br>   *Otherwise, . . .*<br>   *If . . . then . . .* |
| or | Expressing in a different, but similar way<br>e.g. *Rather, . . .*<br>   *Or . . .* |
| | Expressing an alternative<br>e.g. *Alternatively, . . .*<br>   *On the other hand, . . .* |

| | | |
|---|---|---|
| but | Contrasting<br>e.g. *By contrast, . . .*<br>   *On the one hand . . . on the other . . .*<br>   *Whereas . . .* | Contradicting<br>*On the contrary, . . .*<br>*In fact, though, . . .* |

| | |
|---|---|
| | Conceding<br>e.g. *However, . . .*<br>   *Although . . .*<br>   *Nevertheless, . . .* |
| for | Expressing reason<br>e.g. *Since . . .*<br>   *Because . . .* |

*Figure 33: 'Connectives' chart prototype*

*Example 1*    Here is the opening section of a newspaper article entitled *Turning the Alps into a rocky desert*. Beside it, corresponding to the numbers at various points in the text, you will find questions and answers which attempt to make explicit the train of thought underlying the words on the page.

**The Alps are crumbling.** Europe's most majestic mountain range, a symbol of unspoilt nature and paradise for holiday-makers, is in grave danger.

It is a quiet, sly danger which has been creeping up almost unnoticed for years - (1) a forest collapsing here, a landslide there, the odd flood, more landslides. But now it is growing faster and faster, (2) each new disaster opening the way for others in a mounting momentum which is ever more difficult to stop.

(3) Environmentalists declare that even if, by some miracle, the causes of decay could be switched off today it would take decades for the Alps to recover - (4) if they ever did. The gloomiest predict that they will one day end up a silent, rocky desert.

The disease which is gnawing away at the Alps has many interconnected causes. But behind them all is one culprit - (5) man. (6) The fumes from factories, traffic and well-heated homes are killing the protective forests (7), (8), (9), (10). As roots weaken and trees fall, rain and snow sweep unhindered to the valleys, taking with them soil and vegetation and paving the way for more slides.

(11) The boom in winter sports and tourism is demanding yet more ski-runs, ski-lifts, hotels, roads and holiday homes, (12) which means yet more bulldozers tearing into the mountainsides and wrecking the fragile balance of nature (13).

(14) Alpine farmers, whose ancient way of life can hardly be sustained in modern economies (15) (16), are moving down to the valleys and abandoning their lovingly preserved pastures to the elements (17).

(1) *How do we know it has been creeping up?* Because of examples such as landslides, floods and so on . . .

(2) *Why is it growing faster?* Because each single new disaster leads to a few more disasters in a vicious spiral . . .

(3) *What is the extent of the danger?* Very great, because only a miracle could stop its causes . . .

(4) *Are the Alps likely to recover?* Probably not . . .

(5) *Who is this culprit?* We ourselves . . .

(6) *Why are we the culprit?* Because we demand industrial goods, we use vehicles, and we want comfort and warmth in our homes – all of which create air pollution.

(7) *What do the forests protect?* The Alps . . .

(8) *How do they protect them?* With their roots, which hold the soil together . . .

(9) *How do the fumes kill the trees?* The trees become sick, therefore their roots weaken, therefore they fall . . .

(10) *How does this contribute to the 'disease' of the Alps?* It allows rain and snow to erode the soil . . .

(11) *Are there other ways in which we are the culprit?* Yes. One of them is our use of the Alps for sports and leisure . . .

(12) *Why is this destructive?* Because it wrecks the balance of nature . . .

(13) *How is the balance wrecked?* Because too many trees are destroyed for building projects . . .

(14) *Are there other ways in which we are the culprit?* Yes. One of them is our modern economy . . .

(15) *Why is this destructive?* Because farmers cannot maintain traditional farming methods . . .

(16) *Why not?* Because they are not economically viable . . .

(17) *How does this affect the health of the Alps?* Because farmers abandon their farms, therefore the pastures are no longer cared for, therefore the soil erosion process begins . . .

*Example 2*

Here is the opening part of a draft text on a thirteenth century Egyptian scholar, written by an Iraqi student. It is a good example of how the words on the page do not make clear to the reader the logical connections between the ideas in the writer's mind. Below the text itself you will find part of the discussion which took place in a conferencing session (see 6.2.1 *Reading and responding: Teacher to student* (p. 124), and 6.3.1 *Continuing and improving the draft* (p. 131)) to unravel the logical links and clarify the progression of thought. You could ask your students to reformulate the text, using the information in the 'conference' discussion.

**Nihaya's text**

> The encyclopaedist and historiographer Shihab al-din Abu-l 'Abbas Ahmed b.'Abd al Wahhab al Nuwairi, who was born in 1279 AD in Upper Egypt became a favourite secretary of the Mamluk Sultan al Nasir muhammed b. Qalaun.
>
> Al-Nuwairi spent almost twenty years composing *Nihayat al-arab fi funun al-adab* (Aim of the Intelligent in the Arts of Letters). This lengthy work is divided into five parts (funun): the first deals with cosmology and geography (Heaven and Earth), the second with Man (including politics and ethics) and the third with animals, the fourth with plants and the final part with history.
>
> Al-Nuwairi dealt with animals in the following categories:
> I    Beasts of prey (lions, tigers etc)
> II   Other wild animals (elephants, rhinoceros etc)
> III  Mounted animals (horses, mules, asses, camels etc)
> IV  Venomous animals (divided into lethal and non-lethal)
> V    Birds and fishes (in eight sections including different methods of fishing and hunting)
>
> Al-Nuwairi explains how the Arabs dealt with locusts when they became a serious threat to farming in *Bilad-al-Sham* by bringing a special bird called *al-Samundle* from *Khozstan* which he gives a detailed description, which eats the locusts two, three or four at a time and digs to find their eggs in order to eat them.

**Conference discussion**

1  Q: Why mention the book in Para 2?
    A: Because it's the reason for Al-Nuwairi's fame. It was his life's work, and although a lot of his ideas were based on those of other scholars of the ancient world, it was the most comprehensive and original attempt at classifying information about man and the world at that time.

    AMENDMENT: Join the first two paragraphs together, and include the *explanation* for Al-Nuwairi's fame.

2  Q: Why pick upon the animal section of the book for detailed analysis in the third paragraph?
    A: Because it's the most interesting, in that Al-Nuwairi's writings about birds and animals were based on actual observation, in contrast to the other sections.

AMENDMENT: Include the above information at the beginning of Para 3, both as a link with Para 2, and as a reason for devoting the rest of the essay to Al-Nuwairi's descriptions of birds and animals.

3 Q: Why mention the special birds in the fourth paragraph? Is this a new topic?

A: The special birds are an example of Al-Nuwairi's originality of approach in his descriptions of birds and animals. This is to show the contrast with his classification system, described in Para 3, which is very conventional.

AMENDMENT: Make a comment at the beginning of Para 4 on the unoriginality of the classification system in Para 3, and contrast it with the originality of the actual descriptions of animals and birds. Use the example of the special birds being a kind of medieval biological pest-control device as an illustration of this originality.

4 Q: In Para 4, what does the 'detailed description' refer to – the bringing of the birds, or the birds themselves, or both?

A: Al-Nuwairi tells us that it was very difficult to persuade the birds to live in an environment so different from their place of origin, so the ancient Arabs tried to simulate the correct environmental conditions by, for example, making special provisions for the amounts of water which the birds were used to.

AMENDMENT: Include the above information as an elaboration of the idea to be stated in Para 4 that Al-Nuwairi was in many ways an original observer of human and natural affairs. This will help to show the reader the significance of Al-Nuwairi's contribution, and why he is considered by the modern age to have been an outstanding scholar of his time.

**7.2.2 Testing cohesive links**

Besides making sure that the *logical* threads which bind a text together are intact, writers also have to weave various strands of ideas and information into a coherent *linguistic* fabric of sentences and paragraphs. Tackling the areas of coherence and cohesion is a mammoth task, and since they encompass such a vast and complex network of considerations, it would be neither wise, nor indeed feasible, to attempt to cover them all in one activity or session.

Below are some suggestions for various activities which you could try out in a series of lessons. We have grouped them into three sets of types of materials and tasks, some of which are analytical and sensitising in nature, whilst others are based on reconstruction processes. None of them pretends to be exhaustive.

Variation 1: ○
Analysing cohesive
devices in a text

**Materials**

- Multiple copies of a text suitable for analysis of reference devices. The first part of it should be reproduced on an OHT if possible (see Example 1 below).
- Multiple copies of a text with various kinds of cohesive devices blanked out – reference items, connective expressions, lexical substitutions and so on (see Example 2).
- An OHT or copies of the original text.

**Procedure**

1   Give the students a copy of the text whose reference system they are to analyse. Look at the first part of it together. Draw attention to the first reference item, get students to mark it, and then ask them what it refers to. They should indicate the noun or phrase referred to with an arrow (see Example 1 below). If you have the first part of the text on OHT, it is easy to illustrate what you want them to do.

2   Ask them to follow similar procedures with the rest of the text, and check answers.

3   Now get them to work with the second text, where various types of cohesive devices have been blanked out (see Example 2). Their task is to fill in the blanks, and then compare their suggestions with the words the writer used in the original text.

*Example 1*

Text for analysis of reference devices.

> It has been claimed that factors such as a person's 'sense of identity' and feelings of 'group affiliation' are strong determiners of the acquisition of accurate pronunciation of a foreign language. As a means of exploring the meaning of these terms and the role of such factors, let's start by considering how native speakers of a language react to different accents of their own languages.
>
> Suppose an Australian moves to the United States, or a Spaniard moves from Barcelona to Seville, or an American takes up residence in Great Britain. Will the Australian begin to speak with a American accent? Will the Spanish speaker lose the characteristic 'th' sound and replace it with the 's' characteristic of most other Spanish accents? Will the American begin to use different vowels in 'can' and 'can't' instead of the same vowel? It is difficult to predict whether people will modify their accent or not, and, if they do, to what extent and in what ways. Individuals seem to vary greatly. Some seem to be 'impervious' and even after a long time will absorb only some turns of phrase and the pronunciation of a few individual words; others seem very receptive and begin to change their accent almost as soon as they step off the plane!

# The loss of Lardie Moonlight

A few years ago an old Aboriginal woman named Lardie Moonlight died in Boulia, a small town in western Queensland. Her death rated a few lines in the papers, but the full significance of her passing went unreported. Lardie was the last fluent speaker of the Kalkadoon language, a language of such versatility and ingenuity that it stands as a monument to human intellectual development.

It is a commonly-held belief in Australia that the Aborigines have no real language, just a few words and no grammar. Even many educated Australians think that the Aboriginal languages are primitive.

Nothing could be further from the truth. The Aborigines, like all human groups, had highly articulated languages. Indeed, no native language is primitive. All express the complex experiences of their speakers. All have large vocabularies and sets of rules for putting words together in sentences.

The death of Lardie Moonlight was not an isolated event. Every year, on average, the last speaker of yet another Australian language dies and a unique intellectual instrument passes from use as a living language, at best recorded in the barest outline. There were hundreds of different languages spoken on the Australian continent when the Europeans began to take over in the late eighteenth century. More than half of them have now perished and only a score or more will survive into the next century.

*Figure 34: Example 2 original text*

*Example 2*

Here is a text with some of its cohesive devices blanked out. The original text is reproduced in *Figure 34*.

---

**The loss of Lardie Moonlight**

A few years ago an old Aboriginal woman named Lardie Moonlight died in Boulia, a small (1) _____ in western Queensland. (2) _____ death rated a few lines in the papers, but the full significance of (3) _____ (4) _____ went unreported. Lardie was (5) _____ last fluent speaker of the Kalkadoon language, (6) _____ (7) _____ of such versatility and ingenuity (8) _____ it stands as a monument to human intellectual development.

(9) _____ is a commonly-held belief in Australia that the Aborigines have no real (10) _____, just a few words and no grammar. (11) _____ many educated Australians think that the Aboriginal (12) _____ are primitive.

(13) _____ could be further from the truth. The Aborigines, (14) _____ all human groups, had highly articulated languages. (15) _____, no native language is (16) _____. (17) _____ express the complex experiences of (18) _____ speakers. (19) _____ have large vocabularies and sets of rules for putting words together in sentences.

The death of Lardie Moonlight was not an isolated (20) _____. Every year, on average, the last (21) _____ of yet (22) _____ Australian language dies and a unique intellectual instrument passes from use as a living language, at best recorded in the barest outline. There were hundreds of different (23) _____ spoken on the Australian continent when the Europeans began to take over in the late eighteenth century. More than half of (24) _____ have now (25) _____ and (26) _____ a score or more will (27) _____ into the next (28) _____.

---

Variation 2: ○
Unscrambling

**Materials**

- Multiple copies of a text suited to the level and interests of your students, deconstructed into either scrambled sentences or scrambled paragraphs, depending on the length and complexity of the text chosen. Highlight connectives and reference devices which make the text cohere (see Example 3).
- An OHT of the original text, or copies for each group of students.
- Sets of two (different) unscrambled texts. These should be fairly short – perhaps newspaper letters. There should be enough copies for each pair of students to have one copy of each text.
- Slips of paper and text-liners.

**Procedure**

1 Introduce the topic and purpose of the scrambled text, and discuss how one might expect such a text to be organised. A mixed nationality group of students, for instance, reconstructed the *Wedding* text in Example 3 below. They found that, in addition to the linguistic system of reference and cohesion, their concept (or 'schema') of what a wedding involves – the elements and sequence of which appear to be fairly consistent across cultures – helped them to put the paragraphs in order.

2 Give out the scrambled text, and ask the students to reconstruct it. Stress that the highlighted cohesive linking words and reference items should help them to do this. Compare results with the original text (which can be displayed on OHP). Review the process of reconstruction and discuss the reasons for the original text having the structure it has.

3 Now ask students to work with a partner on the two unscrambled short texts. Each partner has a different text, but both follow the same procedure:
   - They write out each sentence of their text on a separate slip of paper, highlighting the words and phrases which they think bind the text together.
   - They exchange slips, and try to reconstruct the texts. They can check the results with the original text of their partner.

*Example 3*

A deconstructed text. The original text is reproduced in *Figure 35*.

**A** Once negotiations have been finalised and an agreement reached, everyone shakes hands on it, and the following evening all relatives on both sides are invited to feast and celebrate at the future bride's family home, and the engagement date is decided.

**B** This wedding-day party is but the first in a three-day celebration of feasting, singing and dancing. The couple then have a few days to recover before the bridegroom's village stages its own party in honour of the newlyweds–a day of merrymaking that traditionally takes place on the Sunday following the wedding.

**C** Meanwhile her father has been saving as much as he can, because dowries usually include the marital home too, and most families buy land and build a house as the girl is growing up. Cattle, cash, a car, certainly a television and nowadays a washing machine too - some, or perhaps all of these can be included in the dowry, depending on the girl's family finances. No wonder boy babies are so popular.

**D** At Cypriot weddings the bride and groom enter the church together. When the service is ended the priest takes the couple by the hand and walks them around a table while nearby guests throw rice, to wish them a "white" (easy) life together, and corn for happiness.

**E** Outside the church the bride and groom are congratulated before one and all proceed to the newly-weds' house to start celebrating.

**F** The boy it is reasoned, will provide for his wife thereafter, so the girl's family is expected to set the couple up for marriage. Excepting those cases where families have a match all lined up, the marriage procedure begins something like this: boy chooses girl and discusses the matter with his family, who take the matter from there. A relative of his - usually the godfather - approaches the girl's family with the proposition, and asks what they will offer in return for the boy's hand.

**G** From this stage of official engagement it is not unusual for the couple to live together, to all intents as man and wife, on a type of trial marriage. If the engagement is to be broken, therefore, the union can only be undone in an ecclesiastical court. Normally though, the marriage proper takes place about one year later.

**I** There is no honeymoon. The couple settle down to married life straightaway and plan a family as soon as possible - naturally hoping for sons...

**K** As far as the bride is concerned, her family have been preparing for her wedding ever since she was born, and a traditional pattern followed since that time. As she grew up, she herself has quite possibly helped her mother and grandmother in the painstaking task of building up an entire linen dowry, for she is expected to provide as many as 100 sheets and pillow cases, 100 towels, bedspreads, table linen, runners, cushions... the list is endless.

**J** On the big day women friends gather at the bride's house to start the cooking - which is no mean task when the custom is to invite the whole village! In the meantime the bride is attended by some of her single friends. Accompanied by music from outside the door they wash her hair, make up her face and help her into her wedding dress. The groom, assisted by bachelor friends, is shaved and his hair cut in readiness for the service. Church bells beckon the couple, and after them a procession follows from the village.

**H** One of the most attractive, colourful, and certainly the happiest of occasions is the traditional village wedding. Everyone in the village is invited, and excitement builds up during the preceding days, but preparations for this day can literally be said to have started 18 to 20 years earlier...

# MARRIAGE LINES

One of the most attractive, colourful, and certainly the happiest of occasions is the traditional village wedding. Everyone in the village is invited, and excitement builds up during the preceding days, but preparations for this day can literally be said to have started 18 to 20 years earlier...

As far as the bride is concerned, her family have been preparing for her wedding ever since she was born, and a traditional pattern followed since that time. As she grew up, she herself has quite possibly helped her mother and grandmother in the painstaking task of building up an entire linen dowry, for she is expected to provide as many as 100 sheets and pillow cases, 100 towels, bedspreads, table linen, runners, cushions... the list is endless.

Meanwhile her father has been saving as much as he can, because dowries usually include the marital home too, and most families buy land and build a house as the girl is growing up. Cattle, cash, a car, certainly a television and nowadays a washing machine too - some, or perhaps all of these can be included in the dowry, depending on the girl's family finances. No wonder boy babies are so popular.

The boy it is reasoned, will provide for his wife thereafter, so the girl's family is expected to set the couple up for marriage. Excepting those cases where families have a match all lined up, the marriage procedure begins something like this: boy chooses girl and discusses the matter with his family, who take the matter from there. A relative of his - usually the godfather - approaches the girl's family with the proposition, and asks what they will offer in return for the boy's hand.

Once negotiations have been finalised and an agreement reached, everyone shakes hands on it, and the following evening all relatives on both sides are invited to feast and celebrate at the future bride's family home, and the engagement date is decided.

From this stage of official engagement it is not unusual for the couple to live together, to all intents as man and wife, on a type of trial marriage. If the engagement is to be broken, therefore, the union can only be undone in an ecclesiastical court. Normally though, the marriage proper takes place about one year later.

On the big day women friends gather at the bride's house to start the cooking - which is no mean task when the custom is to invite the whole village! In the meantime the bride is attended by some of her single friends. Accompanied by music from outside the door they wash her hair, make up her face and help her into her wedding dress. The groom, assisted by bachelor friends, is shaved and his hair cut in readiness for the service. Church bells beckon the couple, and after them a procession follows from the village.

At Cypriot weddings the bride and groom enter the church together. When the service is ended the priest takes the couple by the hand and walks them around a table while nearby guests throw rice, to wish them a "white" (easy) life together, and corn for happiness.

Outside the church the bride and groom are congratulated before one and all proceed to the newly-weds' house to start celebrating.

This wedding-day party is but the first in a three-day celebration of feasting, singing and dancing. The couple then have a few days to recover before the bridegroom's village stages its own party in honour of the newlyweds—a day merrymaking that traditionally takes place on the Sunday following the wedding.

There is no honeymoon. The couple settle down to married life straightaway and plan a family as soon as possible - naturally hoping for sons... ■

*Figure 35: Example 3 original text*

## Variation 3: Testing the cohesion of one's own text

**Materials**

- Students' own draft texts of something fairly short – perhaps the newspaper letters, or short articles and stories they may have written following work in 3.2.1 *Variation 1: Writing a letter to a newspaper*, 3.2.4 *Transforming personal experiences* or the mini-sagas and competition texts in 5.2.5 *Writing a complete text: The mini-saga*.
- Slips of paper and text-liners.
- Scissors.

**Procedure**

1 Here, students work with a partner on draft texts of their own. Ask them first to check their own texts to see that the links between paragraphs, and between sentences within paragraphs, are as good as they can make them.

2 They next scramble their texts, writing out each sentence on a separate slip of paper in the case of single-paragraph texts, or cutting them up into separate paragraphs in the case of longer texts. They exchange these scrambled texts with their partner, and try to reconstruct them.

3 Finally they compare their reconstructions with the originals. If there are discrepancies, get them to consider:
   - whether this was because the cohesive links between the ideas in the original text were not adequate. If so, how could they be improved?
   - whether the alternative version they have come up with is acceptable. If it is, has it changed the meaning or focus of the original in any way?

## 7.3 Checking divisions

Writing, as we have noted elsewhere, is the communicating of a message by means of certain graphic symbols. Amongst the many ways writers have of helping readers understand this message, one of the most obvious is to 'signpost' their text by dividing it into segments, either with or without headings. Graphically, the segmentation of a text into sections or paragraphs helps readers to connect ideas within these sections and to anticipate new ideas or developments between them. Logically, segmenting a text helps readers to follow the development of the writer's thought or argument.

In our experience, the rhetorical conventions of a student's L1 which dictate where paragraph boundaries should be sometimes seem to be at odds with those of English. The focus in this activity is on checking divisions in texts in order to learn and apply paragraph conventions in English.

As in 7.2.2 *Testing cohesive links* (p. 144), we suggest a variety of tasks, leaving you to choose those most appropriate to your students' needs.

**7.3.1
Segmenting**

**Materials**

- Multiple copies of a complete text from which you have removed paragraph boundaries (see the example overleaf).
- OHT (or copies) of the original text.
- Handouts of short extracts from a variety of text-types, comprising sentences from the endings and beginnings of consecutive paragraphs, but with the paragraph boundaries removed.

**Procedure**

1 Introduce the purpose and topic of the unsegmented text and discuss the sort of structure we might expect such a text to have. (The example is the deconstructed version of the original text in *Figure 36*.)

2 Get students to read the text and decide how they would divide it into segments. Try to arrive at a consensus, discussing the reasons for the final choice. Draw attention to how paragraphs are usually developed around a main idea, and how they often, though not always, proceed from the general to the particular. See also whether the logical connective expressions give clues as to how the text should be segmented. Compare the students' decisions with those of the author of the original piece (*Figure 36*).

3   A further task is to work with short extracts from different types of texts (see 'Materials' above). Ask the students to decide where the writer probably began a new paragraph in each extract. Then discuss how a link has been created between the two paragraphs, either through forward or backward reference, or through connecting phrases which develop the idea or action of the preceding paragraph.

You could tie this task in with work on building up knowledge of conventions in English regarding text form and structure (with 3.4.1 *Comparing characteristics of text-types* (p. 75) for instance) by using a variety of types of text to be de- and re-constructed.

*Example*                This is the deconstructed version of the text in *Figure 36*.

---

### Still lives of Liscannor
*George Kavanagh, Nikon Feature Photographer of the Year, records the simple ways of a dwindling community in the West of Ireland.*

James O'Donnell is a fisherman and lives in the village of Liscannor, overlooking Liscannor bay in County Clare. He uses his washing as a makeshift Met office. Strung on a line parallel with the village's harbour wall, it makes a perfect gauge, visible each morning from Mr O'Donnell's window, of the coastal windforce. Hanging limp, the socks, trousers and sensible underpants are reassuring evidence that this is a day to put the boat out. Horizontal, they dance a raggedy jig warning of onshore gales bowling in west from the Atlantic. The weather dominates everyone's lives. "People here used to grow wheat years ago, but the land's too boggy now," says George Kavanagh, whose mother was born in Liscannor. "Cars rust away in two or three years in the gales and rain." Exhausted by nature, the villages of Liscannor Bay face terminal decline, their young people drifting to the cities. In the nineteenth century the area had a prosperous slate industry, Clare slabs being in great demand for kitchen floors. Cornelius O'Brien, local landowner and member in the Irish parliament, built three large towers from which his guests could watch the slate boats sail in from England. Today, barely 2,000 people live around the bay. The fishing community includes a widow of 90 who still goes out in her clinker-built currach, catching mackerel on a long line. The pub remains important for business and social affairs. After a funeral, when the male mourners troop off to the local for a wake, the deceased buys the first two rounds. In Liscannor, the half-and-half shop (half shop, half bar) sells bacon from the flitch, sausages from the freezer and tinned food, some of it 20 years old, from the shelves. The bar has a reputation, reaching Dublin and beyond, for its traditional music played on fiddles, drums and tin whistles. Kavanagh has been visiting the area for 23 years. "Most of the children born in Liscannor don't want to live here when they grow up," he says. "I'm photographing a community on its last legs."

# STILL LIVES OF LISCANNOR

**James O'Donnell** is a fisherman and lives in the village of Liscannor, overlooking Liscannor Bay in County Clare. He uses his washing line as a makeshift Met Office. Strung on a line parallel with the village's harbour wall, it makes a perfect gauge, visible each morning from Mr O'Donnell's window, of the coastal windforce. Hanging limp, the socks, trousers and sensible underpants are reassuring evidence that this is a day to put the boat out. Horizontal, they dance a raggedy jig warning of onshore gales bowling in west from the Atlantic.

The weather dominates everyone's lives. "People here used to grow wheat years ago, but the land's too boggy now," says George Kavanagh, whose mother was born in Liscannor. "Cars rust away in two or three years in the gales and rain."

Exhausted by nature, the villagers of Liscannor Bay face terminal decline, their young people drifting to the cities. In the nineteenth century the area had a prosperous slate industry, Clare slabs being in great demand for kitchen floors. Cornelius O'Brien, local landowner and member in the Irish parliament, built three large towers from which his guests could watch the slate boats sail in from England.

Today barely 2,000 people live around the bay. The fishing community includes a widow of 92 who still goes out in her clinker built currach, catching mackerel on a long line. The pub remains important for business and social affairs. After a funeral, when the male mourners troop off to the local for a wake, the deceased buys the first two rounds. In Liscannor the half-and-half shop (half shop, half bar) sells bacon from the flitch, sausages from the freezer and tinned food, some of it 20 years old, from the shelves. The bar has a reputation, reaching Dublin and beyond, for its traditional music played on fiddles, drums and tin whistles.

Kavanagh has been visiting the area for 23 years. "Most of the children born in Liscannor don't want to live here when they grow up," he says. "I'm photographing a community on its last legs."

PETER DUNN

*Figure 36: Original text*

## 7.3.2
## Paragraphing
## problems

**Materials**
- Multiple copies of a suitable sample draft text, or of excerpts from several draft texts, illustrating different kinds of paragraphing problems (see Examples 1 and 2 below).

**Procedure**
1 Ask students to consider one or more sample draft texts (see Example 1). They have to decide whether the present paragraph boundaries are satisfactory, and if not, how to change them. Make sure that you allow enough time to discuss with them the reasons for either leaving or changing the boundaries.

2 Next, work with a file of excerpts collected from students' own draft texts (see Example 2) illustrating different kinds of problems, and again, ask your students to decide what the problems are in each excerpt, and how the paragraph boundaries might be amended.

*Example 1*

A group of students worked on the sample draft text they first looked at in 6.1.1 *Developing criteria for evaluation* (*Figure 29* p. 120). They had decided then that the text would need segmenting, since it had no paragraphs at all, and that the order of the ideas would need to be changed. Opposite you will see how they decided to divide up the information in the text, using a SPRE/R structure (see 2.2.2 *Variation 5: The SPRE/R approach* (p. 28)) as a guideline.

Their next step was to add and delete information where necessary and rearrange these segments into a more appropriate order, providing suitable links between them. .

*Example 2*

Text A (below) and Text B (below opposite) are two excerpts from students' draft essays on the topic of *Food*, illustrating different paragraphing problems.

**Text A: Daniella's text**

I think that culture and tradition are the bases of the difference between the British and Italian ways of cooking and eating.
I can mention other differences between British food and food in my country, for example: the use of ingredients and the time spent on cooking.
For preparing a dish we don't use over-cooked, frozen or canned food, but fresh food. In fact an Italian housewife on average goes shopping twice a day to buy fresh vegetables and meat. Every small or big Italian town has a fresh food market that is full of people every morning.
Obviously, the taste is complete different using fresh ingredients and I think it is healthier than using dryed or pre-prepared ingredients.
Another relevant fact is the time involved.
We spend a part of our day in preparing and eating a meal - this is because we don't eat just for living but also for enjoying the food, especially if we are with friends.
We are able to spend three or four hours eating, drinking and chatting.
But, as said above, this is a part of our culture and the eating of a meal is considered a rite.

Segment 1:

Woodbury Salterton Society ~~were lucky enough to~~ persuaded the developers of Cooke's farm to allow them to give them the Round House — but where to re errect it.

{ Situation and Problem A

Segment 2:

Stallcombe House farm came to the rescue. With the help of Man Power Services, Mr Dagworthy & the Devon Rural Skills Trust the Round House was dismantled and transported to Stallcombe. It will be ~~is~~ no easy task reerrecting an ancient building & if it weren't for the skills provided by the Trust and craftsmen it would be impossible.

{ Solution to Problem A
{ Evaluation- which
{ could be used as a
( conclusion

Segment 3:

Originally the Round House was attached to a Cob Barn so another cob wall 19' long 2 1/2' thick & 12' high had to be built. ~~A weekend Over 3 weekends~~ A JCB was hired to ~~dig~~ provide clay & over 3 weekends people & bullocks worked to make the cob wall. It is believed this is the 1st cob wall to be built since ~~the turn of~~ early this century. Bullocks trod the clay, oat straw, water & their 'addings' to a cement-like consistency & 3' at 9 time the wall grew.

{ Statement of Problem B
{ Solution to Problem B

Segment 4:

It is said a cob wall must start with the nesting of birds & finish when the last had flown. ~~Hidden traditionally~~ In accordance with tradition coins, newspapers — Guardian, Times, Sun & the names of the builders are hidden in the wall. The next exciting stage awaits another weekend. & the next newsletter.

{ Additional information
which could be linked
to Segment 3 — or
provide an interesting
opening, at least the
first sentence.

Segment 5:

*PS* The Devon Rural Skills Trust is a charity Promoting Country Crafts anything from cob walling thatching to making walking sticks. ~~often over a weekend.~~ Skilled craftsmen are paid to teach & pass on arts such as cob walling & thatching that otherwise might be lost for ever.

{ Last sentence:
predicts result -
possible conclusion?
{ Additional information
which could be linked
to Segment 2.

**Text B: Jassim's text**

In fact food is important things to help humanity in life. Foods problems: particularly in a big country such as England. People are requesting more foods day by day. And they want to buy different typs of food. In some countries in the world people haven't enough knowledge and they eat foods without any information, for example, from where comes, by which company made, which material included. But in England the people and Government situation are different. People had more knowledge and they can say what is good and what is bad they have freedom in their life. But there are several companies thinking thire benefit. In these cases Government and people should be more knowledge about what happen in the society. Health department and agricultural minister should be research these companies, food industrial time by time. Generally there are several strong foodstuff companies in the world which are dominated foods marketing.

### 7.3.3 Cutting-and-pasting

**Materials**

- Students' own draft texts (if possible, two copies of each).
- Scissors, paste and red pens (optional).

**Procedure**

1 Students work with a partner, using draft texts of their own. They should first check their own text, and indicate on it:
   - where existing paragraphs might need to be split up
   - where existing paragraphs might need to be amalgamated
   - where the order of the paragraphs might need to be changed.

2 They exchange texts and discuss any further changes which they think should be made to each other's work. They then get to work with scissors and paste and rearrange the information in their texts in the light of their discussion. Your function here is to circulate and give advice or help where needed.

   We have found that using a word processor for this task – as an alternative to scissors and paste – makes these regrouping and reorganising processes both stimulating and effective, in that it is easy to compare different options.

## 7.4 Assessing impact

Skilled writers are artists with language: they know how to manipulate words and structures both to say what they have to say to the best effect, and to evoke the response they want from the reader. They have become masters of the art of judging the impact of their chosen language upon hearts and minds.

Although few, if any, of us are destined to be ranked amongst the great writers of the world, we can nevertheless train ourselves to become adequate, or even good, writers. One of the vital stages in this lengthy process is to learn how to, as it were, 'commission' language: to choose expressions and structures to create a piece of writing with the force and impact we want it to have.

The focus in this section, then, is on making the right impression with written language. The activities are suited to students at post-intermediate or advanced stages, where there is an interest in vocabulary development and subtleties of style.

**7.4.1 Conveying mood, attitude and feeling**

One way writers have of influencing their readers' reaction is choosing suitable words and expressions to signal attitude, mood and feeling. Even accounts of events or experiences which may appear to be neutral can, in fact, express the writer's attitude towards the subject. On the other hand, an account which lacks any hint of the writer's attitude may be so bland that it lacks all interest for the reader.

Three important areas of language upon which writers can draw in order to convey mood and feeling (from approval to disapproval, criticism to tolerance, happiness to sadness, exhilaration to depression, involvement to aloofness, enthusiasm to apathy, and so on) are:

- **lexical choice** i.e. finding words (especially adjectives and adverbs) which have the requisite associations and implications
- **use of modal verbs** i.e. indicating a sense of doubt, uncertainty, obligation and so on by using modals such as *can, could, may, should, might, must*, etc.
- **use of connective expressions which signal attitude** i.e. indicating a sense of relief, doubt, reservation, conviction and so on with expressions such as *fortunately, undoubtedly, clearly, perhaps, at best*, etc.

The building up of an adequate range of vocabulary and knowledge of the associations and aura of words is a long, slow process. Indeed for some people, native speaker and non-native speaker alike, it is a lifelong pre-occupation, and the tasks in this activity are but a very small step along a dauntingly long road. The tasks aim to get students thinking about ways to expand their basic knowledge of English vocabulary, including using the dictionary and thesaurus to help them. They also demonstrate how, through the use of attitudinal signals, a writer conveys a feeling or mood to the reader, and how, with these signals omitted, more than one interpretation is possible. To ensure that their own attitude or feeling is quite clear, writers have to choose their signalling words with great care.

We have suggested three sets of different, but related, activities, and in each group of tasks, students will need access to a good English-English dictionary to check meanings and usages, and a thesaurus.

Variation 1:
Changing the impact

**Materials**

- Handouts of short excerpts from published texts, suitable for your students' level and interests. These excerpts should contain a range of highlighted words which could be replaced by others *without* change in basic meaning but *with* change in affective meaning (see Example 1 overleaf).

**Procedure**

1 Introduce the thesaurus as a useful aid for writers when it comes to finding the right word: they use it either when they know there is a word which would be appropriate, but can't remember it; or when they feel that the word they've chosen is not quite right; or when a specific word has been used too often in a text and needs to be varied.

If students are unfamiliar with the thesaurus, or don't know how to use it efficiently, choose one or two of the highlighted words in the excerpts from published texts, and demonstrate how to go about finding alternative expressions for them in the thesaurus.

Discuss the various connotations and associations of some of the alternatives suggested by the thesaurus, and ask students to choose one which could be substituted for the word they are considering. Then discuss how using this new word would change the original feeling or impression the writer wanted to convey. For instance, if you chose the word *forlorn* in Naipaul's text in Example 1 below (*l.21*), *Roget's Thesaurus* would give you the following words in the same area of meaning:

> *friendless*, unfriended, lorn, forlorn, desolate, god-forsaken; lonely, lonesome, solitary; on one's own 88 adj. *alone*; uninvited, without introductions; unpopular 860 adj. *unwanted*.

You would then follow up the two additional indicated sections (88 and 860) and have at your disposal the following two lexical sets:

> *alone*, lonely, homeless, rootless, orphaned, kithless 883 adj. *friendless*; lonesome, solitary, lone, eremitical 883 adj. *unsociable*; isolable, isolated 46 adj. *disjunct*; single-handed, on one's own, unaccompanied; unpaired, fellowless; monadic.

> *unwanted*, undesired, unwished, uninvited, unbidden; loveless, unmissed; all one to 606 adj. *choiceless*; unattractive, untempting, undesirable; unwelcome 861 adj. *disliked*.

You might pick out a few possible substitute words such as *desolate, lonely, unwanted, friendless, lonesome, loveless*, discuss their associations and usage and decide that the most suitable substitute might be *lonely*. Finally, you could point out that if you used *lonely* in place of *forlorn*, the sense of pity and hopelessness conveyed by the latter would be missing.

2　Now get the students, in groups of two or three, to follow the same procedure with the rest of the highlighted words in the texts. Encourage them to use the dictionary to help them understand the implications and associations of words they are unfamiliar with.

3　Compare the choices they have made in a later whole class discussion.

*Example 1*　Here is an excerpt with selected lexical items highlighted from V. S. Naipaul's novel *The enigma of arrival*. Naipaul is writing about how Mrs Phillips (the housekeeper in the manor) tries to come to terms with her situation after the death of her husband.

158

Mrs Phillips didn't really know what was happening in the grounds around her. She had no means of judging men, judging faces. Depending on herself now, she was continually surprised by people . . .

5   It was part of her incompetence, her new unhappiness. And it came out again when she tried to get help, when she advertised for women to help in the manor and was surprised again and again to get people like herself, women *adrift, incompetent*, themselves without the ability to judge people, looking as much for emotional
10  refuge as for a position, *solitary* women with their precious things (full of associations for them alone) but without men or families, women who for various reasons had been squeezed out of a communal or shared life.

The first of these ladies came upon me like a vision one
15  lunchtime when I was going out to the bus stop. She was below the yews and she was in *brilliant* green; and the face she turned to me was touched with green and blue and red, green on her eyelids. The colours of the paint on the old lady's face were like the colours of a Toulouse-Lautrec drawing; made her appear to belong to
20  another age. Green was the absinthe colour: it brought to mind pictures by other artists of *forlorn* absinthe drinkers, it made me think of bars. And probably a bar or hotel somewhere on the south coast was the lady's background, her last refuge, her previous life.

How long must she have spent arranging that *violently-*
25  coloured face, *dusted* with *glitter* even for lunchtime on this summer's day! Where – and to whom – was she going now on her day off? So *dreadfully coquettish*, so anxious to please, so instinctively *obsequious* in the presence of a man – everything about her *caricatured* by age, and the caricature set off by the rural setting,
30  the yews, the beeches, the country road.

**Variation 2:**
**Creating mood**

**Materials**

- Handouts (and OHT, if possible) of a text in which attitude-signalling words have been omitted (see Example 2 overleaf).

**Procedure**

1   Get students to work with a partner and give each pair a copy of the text with blanked-out attitude-signalling words. If you can, display the text on OHP as well (see Example 2). This particular piece concerns feelings of respect, awe and fear, but you could, of course, explore other areas of vocabulary by varying the stimulus text.

Ask students to read the text and say what is wrong with it as a piece of writing. They should be able to see that the omission of the blanked-out items has left them largely unable to understand the viewpoint or attitude of the writer.

2 Discuss what kind of attitude they would consider appropriate, given the subject of the text. Encourage them to come up with a range of suggestions, since there will not necessarily be any one 'correct' viewpoint.

3 Discuss how writers draw upon the three areas of language mentioned on page 157 to convey attitude or feeling (lexical choice, use of modals, use of connecting expressions). Spend some time revising knowledge of modals and suitable connective expressions to work with.

4 Then have the students complete the text by filling in the gaps with appropriate items according to the attitude or feeling they wish to develop. Encourage them to refer to the thesaurus and dictionary for help.

5 When they are ready, compare different versions and discuss what attitudes each reflects. If you are working with an OHP, add the different suggestions on overlays so as to make the comparison easier.

6 Finally, show them the original text and discuss what feelings are indicated by the *writer's* choice of words.

*Example 2*

Here is an excerpt from an article describing an encounter with gorillas. In the original article, the writer's attitude was one of a mixture of respect, affection and fear. This is lost with the removal of the gapped items. Students were asked to suggest words and phrases to fill the gaps.

---

Once into the forest we entered a different world: hung with mosses, criss-crossed by fallen, rotted trees and creepers, it was saturated with moisture. Every movement brought down showers of water, and soon we were all soaked.

(1) _____, after only 30 minutes, we made contact with the larger of two groups of habituated gorillas – a (2) _____, almost (3) _____ experience. The old silverback was (4) _____ and we watched (5) _____ as he sat munching leaves or broke off branches in his quest for berries. The whole pack of gorillas moved (6) _____, with the silverback nearly always bringing up the rear. Sometimes he would pause to (7) _____ groom one of the females or a juvenile, and his occasional grunts were answered by females, just out of sight, slapping their chests. Two (8) _____ young gorillas approached us and sucked at our rubber boots.

Watching these (9) _____ giants of the forest, we all felt like (10) _____, and we received a (11) _____ reminder that these gorillas were (12) _____ wild animals when the ranger accidentally stepped between the silverback and one of his seven wives. Within seconds the ranger had been pushed over and dragged backwards by the arm, but (13) _____ he was (14) _____. Having given the warning, the old silverback relaxed and started eating again, and we moved (15) _____ back to the camp.

from *Artist among the gorillas* by Timothy J Greenwood, *Country Life*, May 1988

---

Here are the suggestions from four groups of students for words to fill the gaps, followed by the writer's original words:

| | | | | | |
|---|---|---|---|---|---|
| (1) | Fortunately | Suddenly | Eventually | At last | Fortunately |
| (2) | frightened | frightful | extraordinary | disgusting | memorable |
| (3) | fatal | unique | shocking | repulsive | haunting |
| (4) | enormous | shouting | gigantic | moving | massive |
| (5) | respectfully | carefully | respectfully | carefully | in awe |
| (6) | peacefully | along | swayingly | clumsily | slowly |
| (7) | quietly | gently | patiently | stupidly | delicately |
| (8) | funny | funny | curious | unattractive | amiable |
| (9) | sober | fierce | powerful | enormous | gentle |
| (10) | ants | flies | dwarfs | dwarfs | intruders |
| (11) | sudden | strange | striking | useful | sharp |
| (12) | extremely | really | also | dangerous | indeed |
| (13) | luckily | fortunately | strangely enough | unfortunately | luckily |
| (14) | unharmed | uninjured | safe | dead | unharmed |
| (15) | quietly | quickly | excitedly | quickly | cautiously |

Variation 3:
Using language to
signal attitude

**Materials**

- Students' own draft texts in which they have tried to express feeling/attitude/mood.

**Procedure**

1 Have students working in pairs and ask them to exchange and read each other's draft texts. The objective is for the reader to decide what attitude/mood/feeling the writer is attempting to convey.

2 Readers and writers return drafts and discuss each other's interpretations.

3 They should then collaborate on finding ways of improving the expression of this attitude or feeling. Refer to the three areas of language mentioned on page 157, and put suggestions on the board to help them:

- Can you find adjectives or adverbs which express more precisely the feeling or mood intended?
- Would you add adjectives or adverbs anywhere?
- Can you find any places where you could add a connective, qualifying or reinforcing expression which would help to make the writer's attitude clearer (e.g. *undoubtedly, perhaps, luckily, indeed,* etc.)?
- Are there any places where you could add modal expressions to the verbs to indicate 'certainty', 'uncertainty', 'firmness', 'indecision', etc.?

Encourage them to use the thesaurus and dictionary to help them in this task.

**7.4.2 Signalling an opinion**

Effective writers aim to give their readers something to think about. After all, what is their effort worth if the reader's reaction is a bored 'so what'? The strength with which we signal our opinion, though, and the directness with which we present it, both depend on the writing context.

As students will know from their L1 rhetorical knowledge, certain types of writing demand a formal, impersonal and indirect manner of presentation (the 'scientific report' end of the spectrum), whilst others are expected to be informal, direct and personal (the 'personal letter' end of the scale).

This activity focuses on looking at some of the linguistic resources of English for putting across an opinion more, or less, forcefully and directly.

**Materials**

- Handouts of a selection of suitable, fairly short texts, in which opinions are presented with varying degrees of directness and forcefulness. You could use a selection of newspaper letters, perhaps, or the sort of article in the example on p. 165. If possible, copy them on a single sheet, to make comparison easier.
- An OHT of the above.
- Handouts of Tasksheets 1 and 2 (see Step 2 below) and blank OHTs.
- Text-liners.

**Procedure**

1 Ask your students, in pairs or threes, to read through the texts, considering how the writers have conveyed their opinions. Get them to highlight places in the texts where they feel the language and presentation to be markedly direct or indirect, forceful or restrained.

To make discussion easier, they should make a note of the line references of these places on Tasksheet 1 (*Figure 37*) and then note specific examples of words and structures from these references which support their decisions.

2 In a whole class discussion, ask each group to contribute their findings, and try to come to a consensus about the kinds of linguistic features writers use to make their presentation of opinion forceful and direct, or *vice versa*.

On the board/OHP, compile a collective chart of these features, which should include:

- use of personal/impersonal forms
- use of active/passive verb forms
- choice of words (Anglo-Saxon based: often colloquial and emotive; Latin/Greek based: often academic and distant)
- associations of words chosen (emotive/neutral)
- associations of references used
- choice of grammatical structure (simple/complex sentences; direct/indirect forms)
- use of modal verbs (especially those expressing doubt, uncertainty, possibility, probability)
- variations in normal word order
- use of understatement, irony, juxtaposition, rhetorical questions, exclamatory statements
- use of qualifying or modifying expressions.

Then, on Tasksheet 2 (*Figure 38*) try to match these features with different types of presentation.

3 Finally, ask each group to choose four or five sentences/short sections from the texts, and to 'reformulate' them more/less directly, or more/less forcefully, depending on the original text.

If they do this on OHTs, it is easy for the whole class to discuss how successfully the changes in presentation have been made. Otherwise, simply ask the students to read out their new versions, or write them up on the board.

4   In a subsequent session, you could ask students to bring their own drafts of texts where they have presented an opinion. Get them to work in pairs, discussing and amending each other's work according to how direct or forceful they wish their presentation to be.

**Taksheet 1**

| Presentation / Text | Direct | Distant | Forceful | Restrained |
|---|---|---|---|---|
| A<br>Line refs. | | | | |
| Examples | | | | |
| B<br>Line refs. | | | | |
| Examples | | | | |
| C<br>Line refs. | | | | |
| Examples | | | | |

*Figure 37: Taksheet 1 – writers' opinions*

**Tasksheet 2**

| Type of presentation \ Linguistic features | Types of vocabulary | Types of structure |
|---|---|---|
| Direct | | |
| Distant | | |
| Forceful | | |
| Restrained | | |

*Figure 38:  Tasksheet 2 – linguistic features and presentation*

*Example*  Here are three excerpts from three different writers in the *My country right or wrong* column of the *Sunday Telegraph* magazine, in which they write of their feelings about England.

## Michael Wharton

The 'liberal consensus' which has ruled intelligent opinion in England for forty years insists that exclusive patriotism is not only misguided but evil. Internationalism - "One World" in the cant phrase - is supposed to be the ideal of all but the ignorant or wicked. This affront to human nature - what is patriotism, after all, but the instinct to defend what we ourselves know and value? - seems to be less noticeable in other countries of Europe...

To fear for England now is not just to look back to some imaginary "golden age"... The transformation of England during the last forty years is plain enough to see...

During the last forty years there has been a rapid collapse of religious belief; of morality; of culture and of the arts; a collapse of law and order; a growth of cruelty and brutality. Our hooligans are now the foremost in Europe. As well as yobbery, we have jobbery; there are circles where to be dishonest and known to be so is no longer a matter for shame. "Enterprise" and money-making are commended for their own sake. False science, which regards the whole universe, human beings included, as one experimental laboratory, daily extends its empire, here as elsewhere, almost unopposed, whether in the field of nuclear power or genetic engineering...

An English patriot, who knows what great reserves of goodness, strength and courage remain in this nation, can only wonder how in so'short a time they seem to have been driven into hiding...

## April Robinson

I was brought up to respect police officers and the difference between right and wrong, and I used to imagine that everyone else had been brought up to do the same. But gradually, I have become aware of living in a society which is becoming increasingly violent.

When I first joined the police force it was unusual for a police officer to be assaulted, whereas now, eleven years later, people don't seem to think twice about it. And it doesn't make any difference if it is a woman police officer - there is no sexual discrimination. I was assaulted quite early on in my career, and it quite shook me up. But in court not a great deal happened to the man involved...

I do believe that the British should take more pride in their environment. A pet hate of mine is people using the street as a rubbish bin. I think people should have a basic respect, not only for their own property but for other people's as well. But that attitude seems to have been lost...

They seem to put more emphasis on (material possessions) than they do on human values. Material things have become too important, and people expect to get these things...

A lot of trouble stems from bad influences at home, and television and the press have a lot to do with it as well. Some parents bring up their children by sitting them in front of the television and letting them watch whatever comes on, and yet the more violence you see on television the more acceptable it becomes.

## Terry Waite

There is little doubt in my mind that with the passing of the old prayer-book something vital has gone. One of the links which used to bind me to the past has been broken, and it will probably never be restored.

This is not just a nostalgic cry. It is a recognition that over the years we have, in very many ways, removed ourselves from our history and our heritage. A secular spirit devours everything within its path...

Will no one stand and proclaim the truth that as a nation we learn to know our soul as we understand our past? Will we never realise that we have a positive duty to cherish the artist in society? The ancient buildings of our land tell us a great deal about the souls of our forefathers, just as the drab concrete towers of today indicate a deadness of spirit in our own age.

No matter what politicians say, our nation will not be invigorated until we recover a pride in our heritage - until we recognise what is true and beautiful, and until we learn that as a nation we must care for our national soul. Few are inspired to greatness by economic arguments. The artist through his work can hold before us truths which have lasting significance and which nourish us...

Oh, for leaders with an extravagant vision; for leaders with generous and warm hearts; for leaders who know the language of symbol - who realise that bread alone does not satisfy. Far too much has already been destroyed in the name of progress...

**7.4.3**
**Highlighting the**
**focal idea**

Even though writers might think they know what they are writing about, they are frequently surprised by new angles and slants on their ideas which emerge as they write.

   This activity aims to develop a flexibility of approach to the subject which permits new angles to be exploited and emphasised as the focus for the ideas, and at the same time takes into account the linguistic changes which might have to be made.

**Materials**

- Handouts of a suitable sample draft text (see the example opposite).
- Copies of students' redrafted versions of the sample text (see Step 3 below).
- Students' own draft texts.

**Procedure**

1  Give students, in groups of twos or threes, copies of the draft text to be discussed. After they have read it, ask them to suggest possible themes for this text (apart from the one which may be apparent from the text as it stands). Collect these on the board/OHP.

   For instance, the students who reformulated the sample draft text in 6.1.1 *Developing criteria for evaluation* (the *Roundhouse* text on p. 120) thought that one of the basic faults of this text was that it had no clear focus, and suggested the following as possible focal ideas:

   Heritage 'mania' in England
   Regret at the loss of traditional crafts and knowledge
   Excitement at carrying out a challenging project
   Regret over the 'development' of the countryside

2  Now get each group to choose one of the suggestions for themes, and redraft the text with this idea as the focus. Encourage them to pay particular attention to:
   - expanding and elaborating upon the ideas which gave them the clue to their new theme
   - how they will have to reorganise and perhaps change the wording of the rest of the information to fit the new angle.

3  Make sufficient copies of each group's re-drafted version so that each group has a copy of all the other groups' work (or copy each group's version onto OHT) and discuss each version in turn. Invite the class to comment on the success, or otherwise, with which each group has given prominence to its theme. Discuss the ways in which the original ideas have had to be changed, for instance:
   - how the information has been rearranged
   - which ideas have been moved to the beginning
   - which ideas have been moved to the end
   - which ideas have been expanded or elaborated
   - which ideas have been omitted.

4  As an extension of the above activities, get students to work on draft texts of their own, with a partner. They exchange and read drafts, the reader trying to identify the writer's focal idea. They then suggest ways of making the focal idea more prominent, if they feel this is necessary.

This might involve:

- choosing more emphatic vocabulary and structures
  (see 7.4.1 *Conveying mood, attitude and feeling* (p. 157)
  and 7.4.2 *Signalling an opinion* (p. 161))
- adding attitudinal connective expressions
  (See 7.4.1 *Conveying mood, attitude and feeling*)
- expanding upon certain points in the text
- rearranging the order in which the ideas are presented.

*Example*

Here is the text a Japanese student developed from the general topic of *Food*. She had chosen to focus on the relation of food with season.

**Akemi's text: Season and food**

> Nowadays, there is nothing that we cannot get the food which you want any time in Japan, if you have money. I have really realized that how luxuriant food life we have. In fact, there are quite many shops where you can buy the food from many parts of the world and almost all vegetables or fruit all the year round. However, this is deplored by a part of the Japanese people, because, in the past, the food was very concerned with a season. But it has been disappearing.
>
> Since old times, the significance of the four seasons has been very important for the Japanese. We have spring, summer, autumn and winter which are more definite than English one, therefore we have adapted our lives to each season. Also we had the vegetables, fruit and seafood which we could eat only while a certain term. We enjoyed these foods each season and could feel the change of the four seasons throughout the food.
>
> There is a good example which you can know how important for us a season is. This is 'haiku' which is the Japanese traditional poetry. The most important point of 'haiku' is to use the words or phrases which express the season. This is called 'the seasonal words', which includes many food. Each season has the seasonal words, for example, spring: strawberry, summer: watermelon, winter: pumpkin and so on. We have associated the food with four seasons.
>
> However, I doubt at the moment whether the Japanese children can make 'haiku' or not. As a result of a high technology, we can make crops thrive at all seasons, for example by a green house. Also fish or meat are frozen. Therefore the children do not know how vegetables and fruit thrive or when crop is harvested in the natural way. I think we should consider that this is a serious problem for us.
>
> In conclusion, our lives have been becoming extremely wealthy and luxurious for a short time, but also we have been losing something very important while the same time. In the future, I would teach my children the correlation between the food and season and hope they will be able to make 'haiku'.

When fellow students read her text, they felt that, interesting though it was, there were several other angles which might have been pursued as the focus of this piece of writing:

What we have lost as a result of food 'internationalisation'
The negative effects of Westernisation upon Japanese culture
Regret over how modern life has made us lose touch with the earth
The extent to which food is still associated with season
The advantages and disadvantages of modern food technology and
    agricultural methods

Having discussed these various angles, the students grouped themselves according to the theme they found most interesting and reworked the original essay around this new focus, adding new ideas and rearranging the information they decided to include.

## 7.4.4 Adjusting the style

'Fine-tuning' the final draft frequently entails making stylistic changes to suit the contextual constraints of the writing task. Getting a feel for the effects of organisational, grammatical and lexical choices is therefore an important part of writing, and practice in observing and making stylistic changes has a place in the development of writing skills.

### Materials

- Handouts of published texts to use as illustrations of style, or for reformulating tasks (see Examples 1 – 5).
- Copies (or OHTs) of students' reformulated versions of these published texts.

### Procedure

1  First ask students how they would address (in writing) a cross-section of people with whom they have different kinds of relationships, for example:
    - a close friend
    - a person senior to themselves
    - someone they have never met before.
    Refer to Example 1 opposite as an illustration of the inappropriacy which can result when there is a mismatch between style and the relationship between writer and addressee.

2  Contrast a few texts which differ as regards formality of style and relationship between writer and reader. You could use formal and informal invitations to illustrate the point very effectively, for instance. Or find texts such as Examples 2 and 3, which offer a nice contrast between a writer's actual style and a critic's commentary upon it. Example 4 shows how humour can be based on an exaggeration of a recognised stylistic stereotype.

3  Now look at a text which you are going to ask the students to reformulate in a different style. Use texts such as Example 5 below, where the task is to make the language more direct and less impersonal. Or ask students to think of contexts in which they might have occasion to write to the Vice Chancellor of a university, and reformulate Example 1 in more formal style.
    Refer to the list of linguistic features discussed in Step 2 of 7.4.2 *Signalling an opinion* (p. 162), and add to it, according to the

observations students make about the texts you discuss in this present activity. (For instance, you might feel that more attention needs to be given to the relative complexity of sentence structure in much formal, academic writing.)

4 Later, compare some of the reformulations students have produced, discussing how linguistic changes have created a different style. This kind of comparison can be very illuminating, especially at advanced levels, where students tend to be concerned with subtleties of style.

It is also important to realise that there are rarely 'correct' ways of altering a text, and that several stylistic variants may be equally effective.

5 As part of the on-going activity connected with the gradual building up of knowledge about different types of writing (as suggested in 3.4.1 *Comparing characteristics of text-types* (p. 75)), gather a collection of excerpts from a variety of texts where the style and choice of vocabulary identifies them as specific types of writing (legal documents, formal public notices, academic journal articles, sports reports, charity appeals, etc.). Ask students to analyse the language of these texts using the list of linguistic features compiled in Step 2 of the procedure in 7.4.2 *Signalling an opinion* as a guide to discussing the stylistic differences between the pieces.

*Example 1*

Here is a letter written by a prospective overseas student to the Vice-Chancellor of a university. As you will see, the style – and indeed the content – of the letter is inappropriate to the context, although as a letter to a prospective pen-friend, it is much nearer the mark.

Dear Daivid,
You do not know who I am. So let me first introduce myself. I was very keen to get a penfriend in England. So I applied to bureau here which puts people in Iran in touch with penfriends in various countries. they very kindly gave me your address so here I am writing to you.

My name is Amir daneshzadeh and I am a boy. I am 20 years old and in class 2 of English course in AZAD University of Boroojerd. I am 172 cm. tall and weigh 55 kilos

I enclose a photograph of myself. I have two brothers and one sister By the way, I am a writer too, I sometimes write story books and also I collect stamps and would be very glad if you would send me some English ones, I shall send you some IRANIAN ones in exchange, If you are interested. I hope that you will write to me soon and tell me all about yourself.

Yours sincerely.
Amir
daneshzadeh

The following two texts illustrate a contrast between the direct, seemingly simple language of one of contemporary literature's most influential stylists, Ernest Hemingway, and the much more distant and academic language of literary criticism.

*Example 2*

> Across the open mouth of the tent Nick fixed cheese cloth to keep out mosquitoes. He crawled inside under the mosquito bar with various things from the pack to put at the head of the bed under the slant of the canvas. Inside the tent the light came through the brown canvas. It smelled pleasantly of canvas. Already there was something mysterious and homelike. Nick was happy as he crawled inside the tent. He had not been unhappy all day. This was different though. Now things were done. There had been this to do. Now it was done. It had been a hard trip. He was very tired. That was done. He had made his camp. He was settled. Nothing could touch him. It was a good place to camp. He was there, in the good place. He was in his home where he had made it. Now he was hungry.

from *Big two-hearted river* by Ernest Hemingway

*Example 3*

> If a writer's prose were transparently simple and honest, Hemingway felt, he could leave his meaning implicit and the reader would discern it and even help to provide it...
>
> Accordingly, Hemingway's seemingly matter-of-fact, laconic statements are highly stylised sentences that can incorporate the rhythms and diction of colloquial speech along with archaic inversions of sentence structure and parodies of Gertrude Stein's or the Bible's prose. Their simplicity...assigns a priority to feeling over thought and to action over comment. The result is that Hemingway can suggest, through oblique implication, compressed irony, or understatement, a sense of moral urgency along with a considerable range and astonishing intensity of feeling, while rendering outward actions and scenes with a vividness seldom matched...

from *The Norton anthology of American literature* (shorter edition)

You could ask your students, as a purely academic exercise only, of course, to change the styles of these two texts, making Example 2 less 'naive' and Example 3 less 'scholarly'. Ask them to pay attention to the sorts of structural and lexical changes this entails.

*Example 4*    Here is an illustration, from the *Independent*'s columnist, Miles Kington, of how style is a fruitful source for parody.

# MILES KINGTON
## Language of lawyers explained

It is sometimes thought that Esperanto was one of the first attempts to provide a home-made language. Far from it. This year we are celebrating the 500th anniversary of the founding of the world's first artificial language, legal English, so I am printing today an interview with Stanley Quodlibet, the official historian of the language.

*Q.* Mr Quodlibet, I believe you are the secretary of the Council for the Preservation of Legal English. *A.* I am.

*Q.* Could you perhaps give us an example of legal English? *A.* Certainly. Ask me your first question again and I'll show you how I would have answered if I hadn't been speaking plain English.

*Q.* Mr Quodlibet, I believe you are the secretary of the Council for the Preservation of Legal English.

*A.* Whereas a duly appointed body was set up, initiated or otherwise instituted in the year 1905 for the purpose of examining the history and safeguarding the future of the tongue known as legal English, that body being titled the Council for the Preservation of Legal English, and whereas a secretary is constitutionally appointed to the said Council to aid, abet and otherwise further its activities, I am deemed at this present moment to be the secretary of that body, or at least to fulfil the functions appertaining to that office, having been duly installed in March 1984 by the officers of the said body...

*Q.* That's a long answer.

*A.* I haven't finished yet. And whereas... *Q.* That will do, thank you. Could you tell us the way legal English works? *A.* Shall I tell you in English? *Q.* Oh, yes please.

*A.* It's a mixture of lots of different things. Bits of Latin. Lots of flowery phrases such as "it is my understanding that" meaning simple things like "apparently". A good many double negatives and the occasional quadruple negative. Many words no longer used in English. Many words which sound the same as ones used in English but are actually given their own meaning, such as grievous, malicious, aforethought...

*Q.* Perhaps you could turn a well known bit of English into legal English for us. How about "Good morning"? *A.* In legal English, that would be something like " Without in the least wishing to prejudice the feelings of the court, may I submit that the nature of current climatic conditions is not so inclement that it might not justify a cautious..."

*Q.* Thank you. Legal English seems a very difficult language to speak fluently.

*A.* Impossible.

*Example 5*    This text illustrates the often distant and impersonal style of many public notices. You could ask your students to 'humanise' it.

> **Small dogs may, at the discretion of the conductor and the owner's risk, be carried without charge upon the upper deck of double-deck buses or in single-deck buses. The decision of the conductor is final.**

## 7.5 Editing, correcting and marking

Editing is the final step in the process of completing the final draft which the writer will submit to the reader, and is thus carried out by the students themselves. Correcting and marking, on the other hand, are forms of feedback to the students from the teacher, the one involving the amending of specific points in the text, and the other, the provision of a grade or mark.

Our emphasis in this book has been on getting to grips with such fundamental aspects of the text as purpose, thesis and viewpoint. To this end, we have stressed the importance of seeing language as a tool for crafting meaning. At the editing stage, however, priorities start to change, for here the writer needs to look at how closely the language conforms to conventions of linguistic and formal appropriacy. In other words, surface details of grammatical accuracy and correctness of form *are* now important.

When it comes to correcting and marking student writing, it is important to continue the collaboration which has characterised earlier stages in writing, and we believe that students and teachers should jointly work on the criteria by which writing is to be judged. Even if, for whatever reason, a joint venture is not possible, students have a right to know, and teachers have an obligation to tell them, what the criteria are by which their work is being evaluated. Marks are often needed for institutional record-keeping and assessment requirements, but in addition to this, a form of grading which can show both students and teacher how the writing is developing can be very useful.

However, to be really helpful, feedback must be focused rather than general. Any marking scheme should give more than just a global mark or grade. A differentiated marking scheme, in which writing is evaluated for specific features, will help to show students where their strengths and weaknesses lie, and indicate to teachers where remedial action is needed (see 7.5.4 *Marking*).

**7.5.1 ▶**
**Correcting the**
**language**

Because writers have to achieve a high degree of autonomy and self-sufficiency, it is important to promote ways of self-correcting from an early stage. One way into developing a partnership between teacher and students in monitoring and correcting language is to follow the procedures described in 6.3.2 *Responding to student self-evaluation* (p. 133) in which the students themselves nominate those features about which they are uncertain and wish to seek advice. By using such an approach, we can find out what is important to our students, and since effective feedback must be both salient and relevant, the correction of self-nominated language problems is more likely to be successful than correction of problems exclusively nominated by the teacher.

Inevitably, though, we as teachers will want to draw attention to language items which seem to be important to us as readers. Several points should be kept in mind when we do so:
● Concentrate on language errors which have global rather than local effects. This means attending to formal language errors which interfere with meaning over a broader span than the individual clause or sentence.
● Don't attempt to cover too many repairs. It is quite impossible for the learner to cope with too many problems simultaneously.
This means that it is vital to establish some priorities with regard to language errors. Two criteria may be invoked: communicative effect and

172

frequency. Global errors which detract from effective communication should be dealt with, while those which are recurrent will also usually need attention. It is worth recalling, though, that some of the most frequent errors (e.g. inflections of verbs) are the most long-lasting. They are also the errors which, for the most part, are least likely to cause communication difficulties and, indeed, the evidence from investigations into native-English-speaking readers' reactions to errors suggests that it is these kinds of errors which cause fewest problems. On the whole, readers regard errors that interfere with understanding more gravely than those which, while 'wrong' are superficial in effect. Thus, the omission of -s from the third person singular present simple tense is treated as a less serious matter than a misuse of modal verbs (*must* instead of *should*, for instance), ambiguity resulting from unclear pronoun reference, or incorrect choice of vocabulary.

During a course of study, teachers and students can work together on a checklist of features to be attended to. One such list is given below in 7.5.4 *Marking* (p. 176). It covers elements at all levels: ideas, organisation, language and punctuation. Developed over a period of time, such a list can form a basis for students to check their own work as well as that of others. It is important, though, that once language errors have been noted, the student should correct them. This will mean, in turn, that the corrections should be checked.

Many teachers devise their own codes or sets of symbols for drawing attention to grammatical features, such as the following:

S     =  subject missing
V     =  verb form error
A     =  article error
T     =  tense error
SV    =  subject-verb concord error
Adv   =  adverb order error, misplaced adverb or adverb missing
Adj   =  adjective order error, misplaced or missing adjective
Prep  =  preposition error
SS    =  sentence structure error

Such symbols can be written in the margin adjacent to the line in which the error occurs, and the student has to identify and correct the errors concerned.

Often, however, such coded symbols are insufficiently precise to help students identify the real problem. An alternative is to annotate the students' text with numbers (much as in the first student self-evaluation scheme discussed in 6.3.2 *Responding to student self-evaluation* (p. 133)) and attach a sheet of questions or comments corresponding to the numbers, which you return with the (unviolated) text in order to guide students into making their own improvements or corrections. (An example of such a feedback sheet can be found in *Appendix 3* (p. 183)).

Aids for students to use when they correct language are:
- a student grammar appropriate to the students' language level
- a good monolingual dictionary
- a thesaurus and/or lexicon.

In addition, many language-focused writing books contain language-practice exercises which can be referred to for such remedial work. Indeed, the value of such materials may be less in terms of the original intentions of the author than in their usefulness for repairing language problems.

**7.5.2 ▶
Dealing with
trouble spots**

Ann Raimes, in her book *Exploring through writing* (1987), suggests a comprehensive range of remedial exercises focusing on twenty-one grammatical trouble-spots for students writing in English as a foreign language. While this is an excellent and practical reference resource to which you could direct your students, it may also be useful for you and your own students to create special files of trouble-spots which crop up regularly, using examples from the students' own texts. You could then periodically devote part of a session to dealing systematically with a particular area of grammar/mechanics/usage which causes problems for your students.

**7.5.3 Proof-
reading and
editing**

Proof-reading and editing is the final tidying up of language and presentation before writing out the definitive version of the text. Such tidying up includes dealing with spelling, capitalisation, punctuation and the use of written conventions such as the avoidance of abbreviated or numerical forms in certain types of texts. To bring home the point that failure to proof-read adequately can lead to a (sometimes humorous) mismatch between intention and outcome, you can collect examples of misprints such as those in *Figure 39*, and get your students to spot the errors.

**Materials**

● A sample unedited draft text, either in handout form or on OHT.

**Procedure**

1  Display or distribute the unedited draft and edit it with the students.

2  Make a list of the editing points you have covered

   Spelling
   Grammar
   Punctuation
   Capitalisation
   Word breaks at line ends
   Use of contractions

   and so on.

3  Ask students to apply the same procedure to a current piece of their own writing.

   **Note**: The *Roundhouse* sample draft text (p. 120) provides a fair selection of editing and proof-reading points which would have to be taken into consideration in any reformulation of the piece. If you used this text, however, you would need to point out that such things as correcting the spelling of *re erect* (*l.3*), or writing out *&* as *and* (*l.5*), or altering the tense of the verb (*l.1*), or adjusting the punctuation (*l.21*) would certainly not have priority over the more fundamental revisions discussed in Step 3 of 6.1.1 *Developing criteria for evaluation* (p. 118) or the restructuring tasks considered in 7.3 *Checking divisions* (p. 151).

**a**

**Two thugs pulled the QE2 out of Sydney harbour yesterday, to tremendous cheers from the crowds of onlookers.**

**Sydney Morning News**

**c**

DAVIS, Emily Jane - late of 5, Sandy Road, Chelmsford. A kind thoughtful old lady who died peacefully. Loved by family and friends who knew her will.

**Essex Gazette**

**b**

Princess Diana greeted Charles with a hiss when she arrived at Gatwick yesterday.

**Evening Star**

**d**

It is whispered that the President's long absence from the public eye is due to reported metal fatigue.

**The Standard**

**e**

*Greenbridge is to receive a grant from the government to keep the woollen mill open for another 6 moths.*

**Yorkshire Post**

*Figure 39: Proof-reading slip-ups*

**7.5.4 ▶**
**Marking**

The development of clear criteria which are understood by students and teachers is an important part of marking, as is the agreement on a marking policy among all teachers within the same school. Using a banded marking scheme such as that described below is one way of doing this.

*Example:*
*A banded marking scheme*

This is a simplified scheme, based on that outlined in considerably more detail in Hughey *et al* (1983). In this example, there is a total of thirty marks, with different elements each having a maximum mark according to the weighting they are given in the total scheme. (You may, of course, decide to weight the elements differently.)

Vocabulary:    covers the correct or appropriate choice of words and idioms

Structure:    refers to grammar and word order

Organisation:    is concerned with ideas and their logical and coherent linkage and development

Content:    refers to information

Mechanics:    is the area of punctuation and spelling

This is how the elements are weighted:

| Element | Poor | Fair | Good | Very Good |
|---|---|---|---|---|
| Vocabulary: | 1,2 | 3,4 | 5,6 | 7,8 |
| Structure: | 1 | 2,3 | 4 | 5 |
| Organisation: | 1,2 | 3,4 | 5,6 | 7,8 |
| Content: | 1 | 2,3 | 4 | 5 |
| Mechanics: | 1 | 2 | 3 | 4 |

Maximum possible total: 30

Thus, a piece of writing which is considered to be 'good' on vocabulary would score either five or six marks, while one that was thought to be 'poor' would score only one or two marks, and so on for each category. The total mark would be a composite of all the marks for each category.

The categories of 'poor', 'fair', and so on, are defined under 'Descriptors' in the table below, which illustrates the definitions of categories for the elements 'Structure' and 'Organisation'.

| Structure | Descriptors |
|---|---|
| Very good 5 | Few (if any) noticeable errors of grammar or word order |
| Good 4 | Some errors of grammar or word order which do not, however, interfere with comprehension |
| Fair 2,3 | Errors of grammar or word order fairly frequent; rereading is sometimes necessary for full comprehension |
| Poor 1 | Errors of grammar or word order are frequent; efforts at interpretation frequently required by reader |

| Organisation | |
|---|---|
| Very good 7,8 | Highly organised, clear progression of ideas well linked; like educated native writer |
| Good 5,6 | Material well organised, links could occasionally be clearer but communication not impaired |
| Fair 3,4 | Some lack of organisation; occasional rereading required for clarification of ideas |
| Poor 1,2 | Individual ideas may be clear, but very difficult to deduce connection between them; in the worst cases lack of organisation so severe that communication is seriously impaired |

We suggest the following activities for you, as teachers, to undertake with colleagues who teach writing in your institution, in order to come to a clear understanding of what is involved in 'marking' a student's text:

### Activity 1
Write descriptors for the elements 'Vocabulary', 'Mechanics' and 'Content' in the above marking scheme.

### Activity 2
Apply the banded scheme to the texts given as examples in 6.2 *Responding* (pp. 124, 127, 129).

**Activity 3**
Discuss and devise a common marking policy. We suggest that you begin by asking each individual to prepare a brief statement of what their criteria are for marking. These can then be pooled and discussed with a view to reaching a consensus on the criteria to be applied across the school or institution. If possible, consultation with students should precede the discussion, and the students should be consulted after the policy is drafted so that it reflects the views of everyone concerned.

**7.5.5 ▶**
**Marking**
**collaborative**
**work**

Writing as a group rather than a solo performance has been suggested in many places in this book. There are several problems with such cooperative working: firstly, to ensure that students do actually help each other; secondly, to make certain that everyone contributes to the best of their ability; and thirdly, to assign a grade or mark to each individual which will reflect both their own performance and that of the group as a whole. However, if the individual grade is in part determined by the group grade, then there will be an incentive to contribute to the overall group performance.

The simplest form of grading is to mark each individual's work separately, and to assign an individual grade. Then, the average of the individual grades would be calculated, and each person would receive this as their grade.

An alternative, suggested by George Jacobs (1988), is more complicated and is best presented by an example:

There are three students in the group: A, B, and C.
A, B and C are given individual grades, e.g. 90, 85 and 75.
To arrive at A's score, those of B and C are averaged, i.e. 80.
A's score and the average score of B and C are then averaged, yielding a final score of 85.
Similarly, B's final score would be 83, and C's 81.

## 7.6 Taking final stock of the product

Written language is a tool for giving substance to abstract ideas. Using this tool, writers have the responsibility to see that the grammatical, lexical and organisational choices they have made are the best options for translating their meaning into words. In the activity below, the products of this process are given a final scrutiny before being consigned to their fate at the eyes of the reader.

**Materials**

- Two copies of one draft text from each student (topic or type of writing are immaterial, since the basic principles of evaluation are the same in all cases. The drafts should, though, be approximately the same length).
- Red pens.
'Re-viewing' checklists (see Step 1 overleaf).

**Procedure**

1   Students work with a partner in this activity, but first, each student should note on both copies of their text its 'context' (i.e. its purpose, intended audience and form). Then ask them to read one copy of their own text, with the aim of assessing to what extent they have succeeded in producing an effective piece of writing within the stated contextual constraints. Provide 're-viewing' checklists to guide them. These can be as detailed as you like (see Appendix 2 for an assessment criteria checklist of highly detailed specifications), but should include at least these basic considerations:

**Basic 're-viewing' checklist**
Have I made the theme/thesis/focal idea clear?
Have I chosen the appropriate level of formality?
Have I chosen the appropriate degree of directness?
Have I chosen words and structures with the power to arouse the
    emotional response I want from the reader?
Have I divided the text up into appropriate segments?
Have I put the segments into an appropriate order?
Have I made clear the connections between the ideas in the text, either
    explicitly or implicitly?
Have I used grammatical structures, word order and punctuation to help
    me convey my meaning?
Have I edited and proof-read my text adequately for errors of grammatical
    structure, word order, word form, punctuation and spelling?
Is the presentation legible and clear, and does it conform to conventions of
    written language?

They should amend their copy of the text where necessary with a red pen, or in any way that stands out clearly. (While we agree with Diffley and Lapp – see 6.2.1 *Reading and responding: Teacher to student* (p. 124) – that red pens have the vice of being threatening, they also have the virtue of being noticeable. In this activity, where students are using them on their own and each other's work, the latter consideration takes priority.)

2   They then read the remaining copy of their partner's text, assessing it as they have their own in Step 1 above, in terms of the context noted by the writer.

3   The final stage is for them to compare their evaluations of the two texts, discussing the comments they have about each other's work, and explaining their reasons for wanting amendments to be made.
    Your role here is to be a general advisor, circulating among the groups and giving help where necessary.

4   Collect the amended texts (or better still, the redrafted texts – if students have access to word processors, and have their drafts on disk, redrafting at this stage should not be particularly burdensome) and assess them yourself. Later, discuss with each student any further amendments or improvements necessary or desirable.

# Appendix 1

**Illustration of a structuring process**

In order to demonstrate the sorts of stages students might go through as they think about structuring their texts, we have reproduced below the process whereby a group of Cypriot students arrived at an initial framework for their text on *Smoking* (see 3.2.2 *Selecting and rejecting ideas* Step 1, A (p. 55). Its purpose was to complain about Cyprus's bad record on smoking, and the form of the text was to be a formal letter to their local MP.

Below are the ideas they had chosen to work with from their brainstorming session (see 3.2.2. Step 2 (p. 55) for an example of brainstorming) and the headings under which they had decided to cluster these ideas (see 4.1.1 for an example of grouping ideas into frameworks).

---

**Ideas**

  7: I know it's harmful but who cares?
10: A good source of money for the government
11: Sooner or later it will be banned
12: It causes lung cancer
25: Economy is one aspect
27: Why should other people be passive smokers?
28: Anti-social behaviour
33: Education – anti-smoking campaign
34: Should be banned in public places
35: Don't smoke near children
36: Pollution of environment
37: Pregnant women shouldn't smoke
40: Unfair to non-smokers
41: Passive smoking
42: Places to buy cigarettes should be limited
43: Smoking should only be allowed in one's home
48: Children shouldn't be allowed to buy cigarettes
65: Young people – enough propaganda?
66: Attitudes in other countries?
70: A curse
78: Waste of time
79: Absorbs vast amounts of money in use and ads
80: Public should react against it instantly
81: Production of cigarettes should be banned
88: Society needs to take active role to stop it
89: Stricter fines should be imposed
92: New legislation needed to control smoking
93: Daily broadcasts of anti-smoking ads

**Headings**

A: Public attitude too passive and complacent in Cyprus (7)

B: Comparison of Cypriot attitude with changing attitudes in other countries (12, 27, 28, 36, 37, 40, 41, 66, 70, 78)

C: Reasons why Cyprus government does not take stronger line (10, 25)

D: Measures needed to change attitude (33, 34, 35, 42, 43, 48, 65, 81, 88, 89, 92, 93)

**Note**: numbers in brackets above refer to points in left hand column.

---

They next discussed the order in which they would deal with these four clusters of ideas, and decided as follows (you will note that they changed their headings slightly to indicate their own attitude):

---

A: People are too complacent – why?

C: Government is also too complacent – why?

B: Cyprus is way behind other countries, where changes in public attitude have taken place

D: Measures we suggest Government should take to change attitudes in Cyprus

---

They discovered that they had plenty to say in B and D, but that A and C were too scanty, and needed expanding. They therefore added ideas from their original brainstorming session (see 3.2.2 *Figure 13* (p. 57)) as follows:

---

A: 13: I can't think of giving it up

19: I love smoking

58: My husband has been smoking since he was 13

C: 83: Tobacco industry employs many people

---

plus a new idea:

---

The tobacco industry is a powerful political lobby

---

And to D they added:

---

46: Considerable percentage of smokers have stopped

76: Leftover from an unenlightened age

---

They then discovered that they had not yet included points 11, 79 or 80. Their decisions about these three points were as follows:

---

79 would be included in C

11 would be used as a link between B and D

80 would be used as a concluding point, i.e. that the aim of the Government should be to change attitudes through propaganda and legislation such that people would instantly react against the idea of smoking in public places instead of being complacent

---

Finally, they thought about how to arrange and link the individual ideas under each heading. For example, this is how they decided to order the ideas under B: 'Changing attitudes in other countries':

---

There is increasing awareness of two negative factors about smoking:
(a) health risks (12, 37), and
(b) pollution aspects (36 – would need additional ideas)
Smoking is therefore increasingly becoming regarded as:
(a) anti-social behaviour (27, 28, 40, 41), and
(b) unenlightened leftover from previous age (76, 70)

---

This then led them to point 46 (that a considerable percentage of smokers have in fact given up smoking) as the start of the final paragraph.

During their discussion, they discovered a basic conflict emerging between the individual's right to smoke and the individual's obligations towards others in society, i.e. 'private behaviour vs. public behaviour'. They decided to use this as their theme, namely that the Government should try everything possible to control *public* smoking behaviour in order to change attitudes, and thus *private* smoking behaviour.

# Appendix 2

**A specification for evaluation criteria** The following sets of questions were used by Tony Shannon-Little's Proficiency Examination class in Rome as a basis for evaluating a narrative/descriptive composition:

## General

What did you like best about the composition?
What struck you about it?

## Force of content

Did the content of the composition impress you? (How?)
Did you find it interesting/entertaining? (Why?)
Could it have been made more interesting? (How?)
Was it original in any way? (How?)
How is the writer's opinion/response conveyed?
Does the writer contrive to remain anonymous? (Why?)
Did you feel it was written for someone in particular?
Does the writer establish a relationship with you the reader? (How?)
What impression/atmosphere did the language create?
Were there any changes of style?

## Range of language

1 Is the grammatical construction over-simple? (Examples?)
2 Does the language used contribute to the effect of the composition? (How?)
3 Does the writer use specific vocabulary (or generic)?
4 Is the writer's use of language ambitious? (Examples?)
5 Is idiomatic/figurative language used (if it is called for)?
6 Is the descriptive language vivid? (Examples?)
7 Is the expected style of expression and vocabulary respected?

## Arrangement and development

1 Is the content of the composition within the scope of the title?
2 Is there a progression of ideas?
3 Does the composition move towards an end point?
4 Is the treatment of various elements balanced?
5 Is there a focus in each paragraph?
6 Is it easy to follow the train of thought/ events?
7 Does the writer indicate what is going to happen?
8 Is the construction sometimes too complex or unclear?
9 Is there a *leitmotif* or recurrent theme?

## Mechanics

1 Is the grammar correct?
2 Are there any basic errors?
3 Are there any recurring errors?
4 Where can the grammar be looked up?
5 Are there any spelling mistakes (N.B. common words)?
6 Is the punctuation correct?
7 Is there a range of punctuation?
8 Is the handwriting legible?
9 Do any letters create confusion?
10 Is neatness a problem?

# Appendix 3

Here is the second draft of an essay written by a Thai student on the subject of
smacking children. The teacher has annotated it in several places with
numbers, which correspond to comments on the feedback sheet, reproduced
below after the essay. The student's first draft had previously been discussed in
a conferencing session, the main focus of which had been the ideas and
structure of the text. The feedback sheet, therefore, was intended primarily to
help the student with some of the language problems, as suggested in 7.5.1
*Correcting the language* (p. 172).

**Isorn's text**

Bringing up children to be good persons is a steep① thing to do. It
is necessary for fathers, mothers and parents② to know how to
bring up their children. Some people study③ from books but some
people have their own ways.

I can remember when I was a child, I did many wrong things, my
father and my mother always explained to me what is right or
wrong, but sometimes I didn't obey him or her, they punished me
by not talking to me, sometimes they smacked me④. As well as⑤
in my primary school, when I didn't do my homework or played too
much, the teachers always punished me by caning⑥, these were
my experiences. At that time I didn't understand⑦ that smacking
or caning children was good or not.

When⑧ I grow older and older, I realize that smacking or caning
children is the⑨ way to make children in good discipline⑩ even
though it is not a quite nice good thing⑪.

⑫However, the Ministry of Education of Thailand has forbidden all
the teachers throughout Thailand not⑬ to punish students by
smacking or disobeying⑭ children or students should have been
punished⑮ by smacking or caning if they have done wrong
things⑯, not doing their homework or not in the discipline⑰. It
depends on how strong of their wrongdoing and parents' and
teachers' determinations⑰.

In the real life, parents still punish their children by smacking or
caning at homes⑱, but there is no smacking or caning of students
at schools⑲. However, only parents and teachers know what is
suited to the children, smacking and caning or not.

### Feedback sheet

Isorn: Well done! You have organised your ideas much better than in the first draft, and developed your theme nicely. The ending is also much more satisfactory than it was in the first draft. Here are a few language points to think about:

1. Could you find an alternative word for *steep*? We do sometimes use it metaphorically to mean *difficult*, as you have done here, but somehow it doesn't seem quite appropriate in this particular context.
2. Fathers and mothers are parents, so the word *parents* seems to be redundant here. What about including *teachers* here, since your essay is going to discuss the bringing up of children both by parents and by teachers?
3. What do they study?
4. This sentence has many different ideas in it. I think you need to break it up, grouping the ideas into two or three separate sentences. It might help to think of ways of joining the ideas together more clearly, so that we can understand the relation between them. You have used commas as joining devices, but they don't really help us to understand the logical links.
5. *As well as* what?
6. Here's another place where a comma doesn't help the reader to understand the link between the two ideas.
7. *Understand* is an appropriate word, but you will have to change *that*, because the rest of the sentence gives two alternatives.
8. Can you find a better word? *When* usually indicates a specific time (past, present or future), but here you are talking about an on-going process.
9. Can you be more precise – *the only way, the best way, the most realistic/effective way,* etc.?
10. Instead of saying *in good discipline*, a better phrase would be *well-disciplined*.
11. Again, can you be more specific? In what way is it not *nice* or *good*?
12. Why have you started a new paragraph here? Aren't you continuing the discussion started in the previous paragraph?
13. Think again about the meaning of your verb *forbid*. Do you need *not*?
14. Find the correct adjective form of this word in the dictionary.
15. The tense you've used here indicates that they were not punished for something they had done in the past, but you are actually talking about a hypothetical conditional situation. Change the tense.
16. Are you going to give examples of *wrong things*? If so, can you add a connective expression to let the reader know this?
17. I would suggest using a parallel construction here: *It depends on how serious their wrongdoing is, and how determined their parents and teachers are.*
18. If you are indicating a general concept, use the singular form in the set phrases *at home* and *at school*.

# Bibliography

BEREITER, C AND SCARDAMALIA, M 1987 *The psychology of written composition* The Guildford Press: New Jersey

BRACEWELL, RJ 1981 Writing as a cognitive activity *Visible language* XIV 14 pp. 400–422

CARTER, G 1985 The postcard in *The book of mini-sagas* Alan Sutton Publishing

CHARLES, M 1988 *Responding to problems in written English using a student self-monitoring technique* – paper presented at IATEFL Edinburgh

COE, N 1989 *Student marking code* – part of a talk at TESOL Spain, Barcelona

DIFFLEY, F AND LAPP, R 1988 *Responding to student writing: teacher feedback for extensive revision* – a workshop presented at TESOL Chicago

ELBOW, P 1973 *Writing without teachers* OUP

FLOWER, LS AND HAYES, JR 1981 A cognitive process theory of writing *College composition and communication* 32/4 pp. 365–387

GRAVES, DH 1983 *Writing: teachers and children at work* Heinemann: New Hampshire

HOEY, M 1983 *On the surface of discourse* Allen and Unwin

HUGHEY, JB *et al* 1983 *Teaching ESL composition: principles and techniques* Newbury House

JACOBS, G 1986 Quickwriting: a technique for invention in writing *ELT Journal* 40/4 pp. 282–292

JACOBS, G 1988 Cooperative goal structure: a way to improve group activities *ELT Journal* 42/2 pp. 97–101

LU CHI 302AD *Wen Fu* (prose poem on the Art of Letters) trans. Hughes, ER Bollinger Series XXIX Pantheon: New York

MORGAN, J AND RINVOLUCRI, M 1988 *The Q Book* Longman

PILE, S 1988 *The return of heroic failures* Secker and Warburg

QUIRK *et al* 1972 *Grammar of contemporary English* Longman

RAIMES, A 1985 What unskilled ESL students do as they write: a classroom study of composing *TESOL Quarterly* 19/2 pp. 229–258

RAIMES, A 1987 *Exploring through writing* St Martin's Press: New York

SPACK, R AND SADOW, C 1983 Student-teacher working journals in ESL freshman composition *TESOL Quarterly* 17/4 pp. 575–593

ZAMEL, V 1982 Writing: the process of discovering meaning *TESOL Quarterly* 16/2 pp. 195–209

ZAMEL, V 1985 Responding to student writing *TESOL Quarterly* 19/1 pp. 79–101